THE AUSTRALIAN Women's Weekly

SAUSAGE ROLL MAKER

VOLUME 2

THE AUSTRALIAN
Women's Weekly

SAUSAGE ROLL MAKER

—

VOLUME 2

Contents

Keep on rolling

Homemade sausage rolls make the perfect portable lunch, afterschool snack, light meal or dessert-time treat. And everyone loves them!

While fillings encased in pastry are the most common sausage rolls, you can use almost anything. Tortillas, roti wraps, bread wraps, crêpes, sliced vegetables (such as eggplant or zucchini), all make wonderful casings for savoury fillings, as do hot dog rolls and mini lotus leaf buns. Other flavour carriers for sweet or savoury ingredients, are batters of various kinds (cake, pancake), ready-made doughs (pizza, cookie) or egg-based custard mixtures. The possibilities are endless!

Homemade sausage rolls make the perfect portable lunch, afterschool snack, light meal or dessert-time treat. And everyone loves them!

A sausage roll maker has a non-stick coating, which is best preserved by using non-stick cooking utensils. Even though the machine's plates have a non-stick coating, in most cases we recommend greasing the surface first. Cooking oil spray is the simplest and easiest way to achieve a light, even coating. Use a neutral-flavoured oil such as canola, as it can be used for savoury and sweet recipes. If you don't have cooking oil spray on hand, simply brush the holes with a little oil.

Sausage roll makers heat up quite quickly so don't require preheating. The recipe will direct you when to turn the machine on (and off). Recipes that direct you to line the holes with pastry and fill with mixture, are intended for this to be done while the machine is off. If the machine is hot (or still hot) it will start cooking the base pastry before you finish assembling the elements; the rolls will cook unevenly and won't match the recommended cooking times.

When making multiple batches, turn the machine off after each batch and allow it to cool for 5 minutes. Wipe the plates clean with damp paper towel before assembling the next batch.

PASTRY

We use ready-rolled frozen sheets of *puff*, *butter puff* and *shortcrust* pastries. These sheets are square, measuring approximately 24cm x 25cm. Depending on the brand and the type of pastry, packets contain 3, 5, 6, 10 or 12 sheets. Thaw before using.

Fillo pastry We use chilled fillo pastry, which is kept in the refrigerated section of supermarkets. These paper-thin sheets are rectangular, measuring approximately 27cm x 48cm. A 375g box contains approximately 20 sheets. Fillo pastry will dry out when exposed to air, so remove only the number of sheets you need. Reroll the unused sheets and return to the packaging; refrigerate as soon as possible. Work with one sheet at a time and keep the remaining sheets covered with a damp tea towel. Brush each sheet with oil or melted butter (or use cooking oil spray) before stacking and repeating as directed.

LINING THE HOLES

Conveniently, ready-rolled pastry sheets are similar in size to the plates of the sausage roll maker. For rolls with pastry on the top and bottom, there are two ways to line the machine:

[1] Cut each pastry sheet in half. Position a half pastry sheet to cover all four holes, pressing gently into the holes. Add the filling. Place another half pastry sheet on top to cover; or

[2] Position a whole pastry sheet so the top half of the sheet covers all four holes, and the bottom of the sheet hangs over the handle in front of you. Add the filling. Fold the overhanging pastry up over the filling to cover.

We use the first method, as we found the smaller half sheets much easier to work with; having the pastry overhang the handle can cause it to stretch out of shape if you're not careful.

SAUSAGE ROLL MAKER 101

THE MACHINE

Commonly available with 4 holes; each hole has a capacity of 2 tablespoons. Check your instruction manual for specific guidance around use.

BEFORE YOU START

The machine doesn't need preheating. Spray holes with a neutral oil spray. Line and fill holes when machine is cold, then turn it on. For items assembled first, turn machine on then place in holes. Otherwise, turn on/off as directed.

COOKING IN BATCHES

Between batches, turn the machine off to cool for 5 minutes. Wipe the holes clean with paper towel. Cut batches into separate rolls with a sharp knife.

FREEZING

Most recipes in this book are suitable to freeze. Reheat from frozen in the machine or in the oven.

SOMETHING

SWEET

CHERRY PIES WITH VANILLA ICE-CREAM

PREP + COOK TIME 35 MINUTES

cooking oil spray
1 egg yolk
1½ sheets frozen puff pastry, thawed
1 cup (150g) drained morello cherries in syrup
⅓ cup (110g) cherry jam
1 teaspoon finely grated lemon rind
½ teaspoon vanilla extract
¼ teaspoon almond extract
1 tablespoon cornflour
vanilla ice-cream, to serve

1 Spray a 4-hole (2-tablespoon) sausage roll maker with oil. Combine egg yolk and 2 teaspoons cold water in a small bowl for egg wash.

2 To make lattice top, cut the whole pastry sheet in half. Cut one half sheet lengthways into 1cm strips. Cut second half sheet crossways into 1cm strips. Weave the short strips through the long strips to form a lattice pattern.

3 With the machine turned off, position latticed pastry sheet to cover the four holes. Press pastry gently into holes. Turn machine on. Close lid; cook for 10 minutes or until light golden. Trim the excess pastry from the sides. Carefully lift out the latticed pastry and set aside. Turn machine off for 5 minutes to cool slightly.

4 Meanwhile, drain cherries again through a fine sieve, pressing down with the back of a spoon to extract as much liquid as possible.

5 Combine cherries, jam, lemon rind, vanilla and almond extracts and cornflour in a medium bowl.

6 With the machine turned off, position the remaining half pastry sheet to cover the four holes. Press pastry gently into holes. Turn machine on. Close lid; cook for 3 minutes. Spoon cherry filling into the holes. Position latticed pastry on top; brush with egg wash. Close lid; cook for further 10 minutes or until golden.

7 Serve cherry pies with scoops of vanilla ice-cream.

COOK'S NOTES
Pies can be made without the latticed top. Replace latticed top with half a pastry sheet and continue as directed. Swap cherry jam with any berry jam.

LEMON CURD & BLUEBERRY FRIANDS

PREP + COOK TIME 50 MINUTES (+ COOLING)

6 egg whites
185g butter, melted
1 cup (120g) almond meal
1 cup (320g) lemon curd
½ cup (75g) plain flour
125g fresh blueberries
cooking oil spray
icing sugar, for dusting

1 Place egg whites in a medium bowl, stir with a fork. Add melted butter, almond meal, lemon curd, flour and blueberries; stir until just combined.

2 Spray a 4-hole (2-tablespoon) sausage roll maker with oil.

3 Fill each hole with ¼ cup friand mixture. Turn machine on. Close lid; cook for 12 minutes or until golden. Transfer to a tray. Turn machine off for 5 minutes to cool slightly.

4 Repeat filling and cooking in batches with remaining friand mixture to make 14 friands in total. Serve dusted with icing sugar.

WALNUT PANCAKE ROLLS WITH BERRY COMPOTE

PREP + COOK TIME 30 MINUTES (+ COOLING)

200g pancake shake mix
cooking oil spray
1½ tablespooons chopped walnuts
1 cup (150g) mixed frozen berries, thawed
2 tablespoons icing sugar
vanilla ice-cream, to serve

1 Prepare pancake mix following packet instructions, adding ¾ cup (180ml) water.

2 Spray a 4-hole (2-tablespoon) sausage roll maker with oil.

3 Fill each hole with ¼ cup pancake mixture; sprinkle each with 2 teaspoons walnuts. Turn machine on. Close lid; cook for 8 minutes or until golden. Transfer to a tray, cover to keep warm. Turn machine off for 5 minutes to cool slightly. Repeat with remaining pancake mixture and walnuts to make 6 rolls in total.

4 Meanwhile, make berry compote: Place berries and icing sugar in a small saucepan; stir over a low heat for 5 minutes until thickened slightly.

5 Serve pancake rolls with berry compote and ice-cream.

CHOCOLATE & ORANGE BAKLAVA ROLLS

PREP + COOK TIME 1 HOUR (+ COOLING)

170g dark orange chocolate, chopped finely
220g roasted skinned hazelnuts, chopped finely
14 sheets fillo pastry
125g butter, melted
cooking oil spray

SYRUP
1 medium orange (240g)
¾ cup (165g) caster sugar
¼ cup (90g) honey

1 To make the syrup: Using a peeler, remove rind from the orange. Squeeze orange; you need 2 tablespoons juice. Place sugar, honey, orange rind and juice, and ¾ cup (180ml) water in a medium saucepan over medium heat; cook, stirring, without boiling until sugar dissolves. Bring to the boil. Reduce heat to low; cook, without stirring, for 10 minutes or until thickened slightly. Remove from heat. Cool.

2 Combine chocolate, hazelnuts and ¼ cup (60ml) of the cooled syrup in a medium bowl.

3 Lay a sheet of fillo pastry on a work surface. Cover remaining sheets with a damp tea towel to prevent drying out. Brush pastry lightly with melted butter. Fold in half lengthways, brush with more butter. Fold in half crossways to form a 14cm x 22cm rectangle. Spoon 2 tablespoons chocolate mixture on a short edge of pastry, 3cm up from the bottom edge in a 6cm log shape. Fold bottom edge of pastry over filling, roll over once; fold in the sides, then continue rolling to enclose the filling.

4 Repeat step 3 with remaining pastry sheets, melted butter and chocolate mixture to make 14 baklava rolls in total.

5 Line a shallow 22cm x 30cm oven pan or dish with baking paper. Spray a 4-hole (2-tablespoon) sausage roll maker with oil; turn machine on.

6 Place four baklava rolls, seam-side down, in holes; brush tops with more butter. Close lid; cook for 5 minutes. Carefully turn rolls over. Close lid; cook for a further 5 minutes or until golden. Transfer rolls to lined oven tray. Turn machine off for 5 minutes to cool slightly. Repeat cooking in batches with remaining baklava rolls and butter.

7 Reheat remaining syrup over medium heat. Pour hot syrup over baklava rolls in pan; turn to coat. Cool completely.

***COOK'S NOTES** Baklava rolls can be stored in an airtight container at room temperature for up to 3 days.*

COOK'S NOTES

For a gluten-free version, use gluten-free bread. For a dairy-free version, use plant-based milk and cream. Swap cream for greek yoghurt, if you prefer.

FRENCH TOAST ROLLS

PREP + COOK TIME 30 MINUTES (+ COOLING)

2 eggs
½ cup (125ml) milk
2 teaspoons vanilla extract
½ teaspoon ground cinnamon, plus extra to serve
cooking oil spray
12 slices raisin toast bread (520g), crusts removed
⅔ cup (160ml) thickened cream
2 teaspoons icing sugar
½ teaspoon vanilla extract, extra
mixed fresh berries and maple syrup, to serve

1 Whisk eggs, milk, vanilla and cinnamon in a shallow bowl.

2 Spray a 4-hole (2-tablespoon) sausage roll maker with oil.

3 Dip a slice of bread in the egg mixture, lightly coating both sides. Shake off any excess mixture. Repeat with a second slice of bread. Sandwich slices of bread together on a work surface. Fold to form a roll. Place, seam-side down in one of the holes. Repeat with 6 more slices of bread to fill remaining holes.

4 Turn machine on. Close lid; cook for 8 minutes or until golden brown. Transfer to a wire rack. Turn machine off for 5 minutes to cool slightly. Repeat steps 3 and 4 with remaining slices of bread and egg mixture to make 6 rolls in total.

5 Meanwhile, whisk cream, sugar and extra vanilla in a small bowl until firm peaks form.

6 Serve french toast rolls warm with cream, berries and maple syrup, and dusted with extra cinnamon.

BLUEBERRY BOSTOK

Pronounced BOH-stock, this French pastry was devised to use up day-old brioche.

PREP + COOK TIME 30 MINUTES (+ COOLING)

100g butter, softened
½ cup (110g) caster sugar
½ teaspoon vanilla extract
2 eggs
1 cup (120g) almond meal
2 tablespoons self-raising flour
12 brioche hot dog rolls (840g)
250g blueberries
cooking oil spray
¼ cup (20g) flaked almonds
icing sugar, to serve

1 Beat butter, caster sugar, vanilla, eggs, almond meal and flour in a bowl with an electric mixer until smooth.

2 Split brioche rolls horizontally without cutting all the way through. Spread a heaped tablespoon of almond mixture over the cut base of each brioche, then top with blueberries. Sandwich brioche gently together to close.

3 Spray a 4-hole (2-tablespoon) sausage roll maker with oil.

4 Place four filled brioche rolls in holes. Spray tops with oil; sprinkle each with 1 teaspoon flaked almonds. Turn machine on. Close lid; cook for 8 minutes or until filling is cooked through and golden brown. Transfer to a wire rack. Turn machine off for 5 minutes to cool slightly.

5 Repeat cooking in batches with remaining filled brioche rolls, spray oil and almonds. Serve dusted with icing sugar.

COOK'S NOTES
Marshmallow fluff is available in the international aisle of supermarkets or at independent grocers. You will need 2 limes for this recipe.

KEY LIME PIES

PREP + COOK TIME 40 MINUTES

cooking oil spray
1 sheet frozen shortcrust pastry, thawed
2 egg yolks
200g tube condensed milk
2 teaspoons grated lime rind
¼ cup (60ml) lime juice
213g jar marshmallow fluff spread

1 Spray a 4-hole (2-tablespoon) sausage roll maker with oil.

2 Cut pastry sheet in half. With the machine turned off, position a half pastry sheet to cover the four holes. Press pastry gently into holes. Turn machine on. Close lid; cook for 9 minutes or until light golden.

3 Meanwhile, whisk egg yolks, condensed milk, 1½ teaspoons of the lime rind and the lime juice in a medium bowl until smooth.

4 Lift the lid. Using a teaspoon gently flatten the pastry into the holes. Fill each hole with 1½ tablespoons of lime filling. Close lid; cook for 7 minutes or until pastry is golden and filling is just set. Turn machine off for 5 minutes, leaving pies in machine to cool slightly. Transfer pies to a wire rack to cool.

5 Repeat steps 2 and 4 with remaining half pastry sheet and lime filling to make 8 pies in total. Use a sharp knife to cut batches into separate pies. Refrigerate pies for 15 minutes or until completely cool.

6 Place marshmallow fluff in a piping bag fitted with a fluted tube. Just before serving, pipe marshmallow fluff on pies. Sprinkle with remaining lime rind.

ICE-CREAM BREAD FINGERS

PREP + COOK TIME 15 MINUTES

2 cups (300g) vanilla ice-cream, melted
1½ cups (225g) self-raising flour
cooking oil spray

ICING
1½ cups (360g) icing sugar
1 tablespoon fresh passionfruit pulp

1 Place melted ice-cream and flour in a medium bowl; stir gently until combined.

2 Spray a 4-hole (2-tablespoon) sausage roll maker with oil.

3 Fill each hole with ¼ cup ice-cream mixture. Turn machine on. Close lid; cook for 5 minutes or until golden brown. Transfer to a wire rack. Turn machine off for 5 minutes to cool slightly. Repeat with remaining ice-cream mixture to make 8 ice-cream bread fingers in total.

4 To make the icing, stir ingredients in a small bowl until well combined, adding a little water if necessary.

5 Just before serving, spoon icing over each ice-cream bread finger.

ICE-CREAM BREAD FINGER VARIATIONS

FAIRY BREAD

Make Ice-cream Bread Fingers (recipe page 24) as directed in step1, stirring through ⅓ cup 100's and 1000's. Cook as directed in step 3. Make icing replacing passionfruit pulp with milk. Spread the icing over each ice-cream bread finger; top each with an extra ½ teaspoon 100's and 1000's.

CHOC & NUTELLA

Make Ice-cream Bread Fingers (recipe page 24), replacing vanilla ice-cream with chocolate ice-cream. Cook as directed in step 3. Omit icing. Instead spread 2 teaspoons Nutella over each ice-cream bread fnger; top each with 2 teaspoons chopped roasted hazelnuts.

CARAMEL CRUNCH

Make Ice-cream Bread Fingers (recipe page 24), replacing vanilla ice-cream with Caramello ice-cream. Cook as directed in step 3. Omit icing. Instead spread 2 teaspoons dulce de leche over each ice-cream bread finger; top with 2 teaspoons chopped chocolate-coated honeycomb bar.

S'MORES COOKIE PIES

PREP + COOK TIME 25 MINUTES

cooking oil spray
300g bought cookie dough, at room temperature
½ cup (80g) milk chocolate chunks, plus extra to serve
¾ cup (40g) mini marshmallows

1 Spray a 4-hole (2-tablespoon) sausage roll maker with oil.

2 With the machine turned off, place 1 heaped tablespoon of cookie dough into each hole, pressing gently to form the cookie base. Fill holes with half the chocolate and half the marshmallows.

3 Turn machine on. Close lid; cook for 4 minutes or until the cookie base is golden and filling is melted. Turn machine off for 5 minutes, leaving pies in the machine to cool slightly. Transfer to a wire rack.

4 Repeat steps 2 and 3 with remaining cookie dough, chocolate and marshmallows to make 8 pies in total. Use a sharp knife to cut batches into separate pies.

5 Serve s'mores cookie pies warm, topped with exra chocolate.

***COOK'S NOTES** For the chocolate chunks, simply cut a block or bar of milk chocolate into small chunks.*

SRI LANKAN COCONUT CRÊPE ROLLS

PREP + COOK TIME 30 MINUTES (+ COOLING)

2 cups (160g) desiccated coconut
¼ cup (60ml) coconut milk
1 cup (220g) firmly packed brown sugar
1 teaspoon ground cardamom
½ teaspoon ground cinnamon
½ teaspoon fine sea salt
1 cup finely chopped pineapple
8 frozen crêpes, thawed
cooking oil spray
tropical fruit, to serve

1 Place desiccated coconut in a medium bowl. Heat coconut milk in a small microwave-safe jug on MEDIUM (50%) for 20 seconds or until warm. Pour over coconut; stir to combine. Stand for 5 minutes.

2 Stir the sugar, spices, salt and 2 tablespoons water in a medium saucepan over low-medium heat until sugar dissolves and a syrup forms. Add two-thirds of the syrup to the coconut mixture with the pineapple; stir to combine.

3 Warm crêpes in microwave on HIGH (100%) for 20 seconds. Place a crêpe on a work surface. Place ¼ cup of coconut pineapple mixture in a 10cm log shape in the centre of the crêpe. Fold in the sides. Roll from the bottom edge to enclose the filling. Repeat with remaining crêpes and coconut pineapple mixture to make 8 rolls in total.

4 Spray a 4-hole (2-tablespoon) sausage roll maker with oil.

5 Place four filled crêpe rolls, seam-side down in holes. Close lid. Cook for 6 minutes or until golden. Transfer to a wire rack. Turn machine off for 5 minutes to cool slightly. Repeat with remaining filled crêpe rolls.

6 Serve crêpe rolls warm with tropical fruit and remaining syrup.

COOK'S NOTES

Leaving the coconut to stand in warm liquid for 5 minutes allows it to rehydrate. Warming the crêpes in the microwave makes them more pliable for rolling.

CHOCOLATE CHIP COOKIES

PREP + COOK TIME 40 MINUTES

485g packet choc chip cookie mix
1 egg
100g butter, melted
cooking oil spray
22 Maltesers (45g)

1 Place choc chip cookie mix in a medium bowl with egg and melted butter; stir until combined.

2 Spray a 4-hole (2-tablespoon) sausage roll maker with oil.

3 Roll tablespoons of cookie mixture into balls; you will have 22 balls. Fill each hole with 2 choc chip balls leaving a gap between each ball. Press a Malteser into each ball. Turn machine on. Close lid; cook for 12 minutes or until firm and golden brown. Turn machine off. Lift the lid; leave cookies in the machine for 2 minutes to cool. Transfer cookies to a wire rack.

4 Repeat step 3 in batches with remaining choc chip balls and Maltesers. Separate cookies when cool.

***COOK'S NOTES** Crisp or chewy? If you would like a chewy textured cookie, reduce the cooking time to 10 minutes.*

PECAN PIES

PREP + COOK TIME 35 MINUTES (+ COOLING)

cooking oil spray
1 sheet frozen shortcrust pastry, thawed
1 egg
⅓ cup (80ml) maple syrup, plus extra to serve
20g butter, melted
2 tablespoons brown sugar
1 teaspoon vanilla extract
¼ teaspoon ground cinnamon
1 tablespoon bourbon (optional)
¾ cup (80g) pecans, roasted, chopped coarsely
16 pecan halves, roasted
⅔ cup (160ml) thickened cream
2 teaspoons icing sugar

1 Spray a 4-hole (2-tablespoon) sausage roll maker with oil.

2 Cut pastry sheet in half. With the machine turned off, position a half pastry sheet to cover the four holes. Press pastry gently into holes. Turn machine on. Close lid; cook for 9 minutes or until light golden.

3 Meanwhile, whisk egg, maple syrup, butter, brown sugar, vanilla, cinnamon and bourbon in a medium bowl. Stir in chopped pecans.

4 Lift the lid. Using a teaspoon gently flatten the pastry into the holes. Fill each hole with 1 tablespoon of pecan mixture. Top each pie with 2 pecan halves. Close lid; cook pies for 8 minutes or until pastry is golden and filling is just set. Turn machine off for 5 minutes, leaving pies in machine to cool slightly. Transfer pies to a wire rack.

5 Repeat steps 1, 2 and 4 with remaining half pastry sheet, pecan mixture and pecan halves to make 8 pies in total. Use a sharp knife to cut batches into separate pies.

6 Meanwhile, whisk cream and icing sugar to firm peaks in a medium bowl.

7 Serve pies topped with whipped cream and extra maple syrup.

COOK'S NOTES

Fruit can be replaced with chopped roasted skinless hazelnuts or blanched almonds. Serve calzone with vanilla ice-cream or gelato for dessert.

NUTELLA & FRUIT CALZONE

PREP + COOK TIME 15 MINUTES

250g pizza dough ball, at room temperature
cooking oil spray
⅓ cup (110g) Nutella
icing sugar, to serve

PICK-YOUR-FRUIT
4 strawberries, halved
1 small banana (130g), halved then cut into 10cm strips
½ cup (75g) blueberries

1 Turn dough onto a lightly oiled surface and cut into four equal portions. Roll each portion into a 14cm square.

2 Spread 1 tablespoon of the Nutella in a 10cm strip in the middle of the square. Arrange your choice of fruit (strawberry, banana or blueberries) on top of the Nutella. Fold bottom edge of dough over filling and roll once. Fold in the sides, then continue rolling to enclose the filling. Repeat with remaining dough squares, Nutella and fruit.

3 Spray a 4-hole (2-tablespoon) sausage roll maker with oil. Turn machine on.

4 Place calzone in holes; spray tops with oil. Close lid; cook for 7 minutes or until dough is puffed, golden and cooked through.

5 Serve calzone warm, dusted with icing sugar.

MARS BAR ROLLS

PREP + COOK TIME 25 MINUTES

cooking oil spray
1 sheet frozen puff pastry, thawed
4 x 53g Mars bars
icing sugar and ice-cream, to serve

1 Spray a 4-hole (2-tablespoon) sausage roll maker with oil.

2 Cut pastry sheet in half. With machine turned off, position a half pastry sheet to cover the four holes. Press pastry gently into holes. Place a Mars bar in each hole. Place remaining half pastry sheet on top to cover. Press around each hole to seal the sides.

3 Turn machine on. Close lid; cook for 10 minutes or until golden. Turn machine off. Lift the lid; leave rolls in machine for 5 minutes to cool slightly. Transfer rolls to a wire rack; cool for at least another 5 minutes. Use a sharp knife to cut into separate rolls.

4 Serve rolls warm, dusted with icing sugar and with ice-cream.

SALTED PEANUT BUTTER TARTS

PREP + COOK TIME 1 HOUR (+ COOLING)

½ cup (180g) honey, plus extra to serve
¼ cup (55g) caster sugar
¼ cup (70g) smooth peanut butter
¼ teaspoon salt
2 eggs
1 teaspoon vanilla extract
cooking oil spray
1½ sheets frozen shortcrust pastry, thawed
¼ cup (35g) roasted peanuts, chopped, plus extra to serve

BOURBON CREAM

1 cup (250ml) thickened cream
2 tablespoons icing sugar
2 tablespoons bourbon whiskey

1 Beat honey, sugar, peanut butter and salt in a large bowl with an electric mixer until smooth. Beat in eggs and vanilla until combined.

2 Spray a 4-hole (2-tablespoon) sausage roll maker with oil.

3 Cut whole pastry sheet in half. With the machine turned off, position a half pastry sheet to cover the four holes. Press pastry gently into holes. Fill each hole with 1½ tablespoons of peanut butter mixture. Top each with 1 teaspoon chopped peanuts.

4 Turn machine on. Close lid; cook for 14 minutes or until pastry is golden. Transfer to a wire rack. Turn machine off for 5 minutes to cool slightly.

5 Repeat steps 3 and 4 in batches with remaining half pastry sheets, peanut butter mixture and chopped peanuts to make 12 tarts in total. Use a sharp knife to cut batches into separate tarts.

6 Meanwhile, to make bourbon cream: Beat cream and sifted icing sugar in a medium bowl with an electric mixer until soft peaks form. Whisk in the bourbon.

7 Serve peanut butter tarts topped with bourbon cream, extra honey and extra chopped peanuts.

ORANGE YUM YUMS

PREP + COOK TIME 1 HOUR 30 MINUTES (+ STANDING & COOLING)

1½ cups (240g) bread flour
1 tablespoon caster sugar
2 teaspoons (7g) instant yeast
½ teaspoon salt
40g cold unsalted butter, chopped into 5mm pieces
1 egg, beaten lightly
2 cups (320g) icing sugar
¼ cup (60ml) milk
1 tablespoon finely grated orange rind

1 Combine flour, caster sugar, yeast and salt in a large bowl. Stir through the butter. Add egg and ½ cup (125ml) lukewarm water; stir until combined. Knead in the bowl for 2 minutes or until smooth. Cover bowl. Stand in a warm place for 30 minutes or until doubled in size.

2 Turn dough out onto a floured surface. Roll out to a 25cm x 30cm rectangle. Fold the bottom third of the dough up to meet in the middle, then fold the top third down to create three layers of dough. Roll out to a 15cm x 30cm rectangle. Repeat the folding and rolling process two more times.

3 Cut the dough from the short side into 18 x 1.5cm-wide strips. Take 2 strips and twist together. Press firmly at each end to secure. Place on an oven tray lined with baking paper. Cover; stand for 30 minutes or until nearly doubled in size.

4 Spray a 4-hole (2-tablespoon) sausage roll maker with oil. Place one yum yum in each hole. Turn machine on. Close lid; cook for 7 minutes. Carefully turn yum yums over. Close lid; cook for a further 7 minutes or until golden. Transfer to a wire rack. Turn machine off for 5 minutes to cool slightly. Repeat cooking in batches with remaining yum yums.

5 Meanwhile, whisk icing sugar and milk together in a medium bowl until smooth.

6 Dip yum yums in icing to completely coat. Transfer to a wire rack until set. Sprinkle with orange rind.

COOK'S NOTES

If you find the dough a little dry, add extra water 1 tablespoon at a time. For a different citrus flavour, swap the grated orange rind for lemon or lime rind.

CHERRY CLAFOUTIS TARTS

PREP + COOK TIME 40 MINUTES

1 cup (125g) frozen cherries
½ cup (75g) plain flour
½ cup (110g) caster sugar
2 eggs, beaten lightly
½ cup (125ml) thickened cream
1 teaspoon vanilla extract
1 teaspoon finely grated lemon rind
cooking oil spray
crème fraîche, to serve

CHERRY SAUCE

2 cups (250g) frozen cherries, thawed
2 tablespoons caster sugar
1 teaspoon lemon juice

1 Place frozen cherries on a paper-towel-lined tray to thaw. Pat dry.

2 Combine flour, sugar, egg, cream, vanilla and rind in a medium bowl until smooth.

3 Spray a 4-hole (2-tablespoon) sausage roll maker with oil.

4 With machine turned off, pour ¼ cup of batter into each hole, then add a few cherries per hole. Turn machine on. Close lid; cook for 12 minutes or until lightly golden. Turn machine off, leaving tarts in machine for 5 minutes to cool slightly. Transfer to a wire rack. Repeat with remaining batter and cherries to make 8 tarts in total.

5 Meanwhile, to make cherry sauce: Stir cherries and sugar in a small saucepan over medium heat without boiling until sugar dissolves. Cook for 6 minutes or until thickened slightly.

6 Serve clafoutis tarts with crème fraîche and cherry sauce.

BOUNTIFUL BARS

PREP + COOK TIME 35 MINUTES (+ COOLING & REFRIGERATION)

2½ cups (190g) shredded coconut, plus extra for decorating
¼ cup (30g) almond meal
¼ teaspoon fine salt
2 egg whites
½ cup (110g) caster sugar
1 teaspoon vanilla extract
cooking oil spray
200g dark chocolate Melts
1 tablespoon coconut oil

1 Combine shredded coconut, almond meal and salt in a large bowl.

2 Beat egg whites in a medium bowl with an electric mixer until soft peaks form. Gradually add the sugar 1 tablespoon at a time, beating until sugar has dissolved after each addition and mixture is thick and glossy. Whisk in vanilla.

3 Gently fold egg white mixture into coconut mixture.

4 Spray a 4-hole (2-tablespoon) sausage roll maker with oil.

5 Fill each hole with ⅓ cup coconut mixture. Turn machine on. Close lid. Cook for 7 minutes or until golden brown. Turn machine off. Lift the lid; leave bars in machine for 5 minutes to cool. Transfer bars to a wire rack. Repeat with remaining coconut mixture to make 6 bars in total.

6 Meanwhile, place chocolate and coconut oil in a microwave-safe bowl. Microwave on MEDIUM (50%), in 20-second bursts until melted and smooth.

7 Place a wire rack over a baking tray. Dip bars in melted chocolate mixture. Shake gently for any excess chocolate to drip back into the bowl then place on wire rack. Sprinkle with extra coconut. Refrigerate for 20 minutes or until chocolate is set.

COOK'S NOTES

Letting the coconut bars cool for 5 minutes in the machine allows the bars to firm up before you lift them out.

COOK'S NOTES

Don't be tempted to bite into these until they've cooled on the rack for 10 minutes as the centre will be boiling hot. Double the recipe for a bigger batch.

FRUIT MINCE PIE ROLLS WITH BRANDY CREAM

PREP + COOK TIME 20 MINUTES (+ COOLING & STANDING)

cooking oil spray
1 egg yolk
1 sheet frozen shortcrust pastry, thawed
410g jar fruit mince
2 teaspoons white sugar

BRANDY CREAM
1 cup (250ml) thickened cream
2 tablespoons icing sugar
¼ cup (60ml) brandy

1 Spray a 4-hole (2-tablespoon) sausage roll maker with oil. Combine egg yolk and 2 teaspoons cold water in a small bowl for egg wash.

2 Cut pastry sheet in half. With the machine turned off, position a half pastry sheet to cover the four holes. Fill each hole with a quarter of the fruit mince. Place remaining half pastry sheet on top to cover. Press around each hole to seal the sides. Brush rolls with egg wash. Sprinkle with sugar.

3 Turn machine on. Close lid. Cook for 12 minutes or until golden and crisp. Turn machine off. Lift the lid; leave rolls in the machine for 5 minutes to cool slightly. Transfer rolls to a wire rack to cool for at least another 10 minutes. Use a sharp knife to cut into separate rolls.

4 Meanwhile, to make brandy cream: Beat cream and sifted icing sugar in a medium bowl with an electric mixer until soft peaks form. Whisk in the brandy.

5 Serve fruit mince pies hot or cold with brandy cream.

RASPBERRY & APPLE STRUDEL

PREP + COOK TIME 55 MINUTES (+ COOLING)

1 cup (150g) frozen raspberries
150g butter, chopped
1 teaspoon ground cinnamon
⅓ cup (25g) breadcrumbs (made from day-old bread)
385g can apple pie slices, chopped coarsely
1 tablespoon icing sugar, plus extra to serve
1 teaspoon cornflour
8 sheets fillo pastry
cooking oil spray
custard, to serve

1 Place raspberries on a paper-towel-lined tray to thaw. Pat dry.

2 Melt 70g of the butter in a medium frying pan over medium-high heat. Add cinnamon and breadcrumbs; cook, stirring, for 3 minutes or until breadcrumbs are golden brown. Transfer to a large bowl; stir in raspberries, apple pie slices, icing sugar and cornflour. Cool.

3 Wipe frying pan clean. Melt remaining butter over low heat.

4 Lay a sheet of fillo pastry on a work surface. Cover remaining sheets with a damp tea towel to prevent drying out. Brush pastry lightly with melted butter. Top with another sheet of fillo, brush with more butter. Repeat layering with 2 more sheets and more butter. Spoon half the fruit mixture along one long edge of the pastry stack. Roll up tightly to form a log. Cut log into four equal strudels. Repeat with remaining pastry sheets, more butter and fruit mixture to make 8 strudels in total.

5 Spray a 4-hole (2-tablespoon) sausage roll maker with oil. Turn machine on.

6 Place four strudels, seam-side down, in holes. Brush tops with more melted butter. Close lid; cook for 7 minutes. Carefully turn strudels over. Close lid; cook for another 7 minutes or until golden. Transfer to a wire rack. Turn machine off for 5 minutes to cool slightly. Repeat cooking with remaining strudels.

7 Serve strudels dusted with icing sugar and with custard.

COOK'S NOTES

Save the cinnamon sugar and icing sugar sachets from the packet mix for another recipe. Pearl sugar (also known as nib sugar) is popular in Europe on baked goods. You will find it in specialist food stores or cake supply stores. You can use crushed sugar cubes instead.

CARDAMOM BUNS

PREP + COOK TIME 1 HOUR 10 MINUTES (+ COOLING)

520g packet cinnamon scrolls mix
¾ cup (180ml) milk
60g butter, softened
¼ cup (55g) caster sugar
2 teaspoons ground cardamom
cooking oil spray
2 tablespoons caster sugar, extra
2 tablespoons pearl sugar (see Cook's Notes)

1 Place scroll mix and milk in a medium bowl; stir until mixture comes together. Turn dough out onto a lightly floured work surface and knead until smooth. Cover with plastic wrap to prevent drying out; stand for 5 minutes.

2 Meanwhile, combine softened butter, caster sugar and 1½ teaspoons of the cardamom in a small bowl.

3 Roll dough out to a 40cm square. Spread with butter mixture. Fold the bottom third of the dough up to meet the middle then fold the top third down to create three layers of dough. Gently roll the dough out until it is 20cm wide. Trim the uneven sides. Cut into 14 x 2.5cm-wide strips.

4 Spray a 4-hole (2-tablespoon) sausage roll maker with oil.

5 With the machine turned off, fold a strip of dough, cut-side down, making four concertina folds. Place in one of the holes. Press down slightly. Repeat with another three strips to fill the holes. Spray buns with oil. Turn machine on. Close lid; cook for 8 minutes or until golden. Transfer to a wire rack. Turn machine off for 5 minutes to cool. Repeat folding and cooking in batches with remaining strips to make 14 buns in total.

6 Meanwhile, stir extra caster sugar, remaining cardamom and ⅓ cup (80ml) water in a small saucepan over a medium heat until sugar dissolves. Set aside.

7 Brush cardamom buns generously with sugar syrup. Sprinkle with pearl sugar.

MINI BANANA BREADS

PREP + COOK TIME 30 MINUTES (+ COOLING)

6 ripe lady finger bananas (780g)
400g packet classic banana bread mix
2 eggs
½ cup (125ml) milk
½ cup (125ml) vegetable oil
cooking oil spray
warmed honey, to glaze

1 Mash 3 of the bananas in a small bowl; you will need 250g mashed banana. Cut the remaining bananas lengthways into quarters, then in half crossways.

2 Combine mashed banana, packet mix, eggs, milk and oil in a medium bowl until smooth.

3 Spray a 4-hole (2-tablespoon) sausage roll maker with oil.

4 Fill each hole with ¼ cup banana batter. Top each hole with 2 pieces of banana. Turn machine on. Close lid; cook for 8 minutes or until golden brown. Transfer to a wire rack. Turn machine off for 5 minutes to cool slightly.

5 Repeat step 4 in batches with remaining banana batter and banana pieces to make 12 breads in total.

6 Just before serving, brush mini banana breads with warmed honey.

HUMMINGBIRD FINGERS

PREP + COOK TIME 1 HOUR (+ COOLING)

470g packet vanilla cake mix

½ teaspoon ground cinnamon, plus extra to serve

½ teaspoon ground cardamom

¼ cup (30g) finely chopped roasted walnuts

¼ cup (10g) flaked coconut, plus extra toasted to serve

2 eggs, beaten lightly

440g can crushed pineapple, well drained

1 large over-ripe banana (230g), mashed

¼ cup (60ml) vegetable oil

cooking oil spray

CREAM CHEESE TOPPING

100g cream cheese, softened

50g butter, softened

1½ cups (240g) icing sugar

1 teaspoon grated lemon rind

1 Combine cake mix, spices, walnuts and coconut in the bowl of an electric mixer. Mix the egg, pineapple, mashed banana and vegetable oil in a jug; add to the flour mixture. Beat on low speed until combined. Increase speed to medium; beat for 2 minutes.

2 Spray a 4-hole (2-tablespoon) sausage roll maker with oil.

3 Fill each hole with ¼ cup cake mixture. Turn machine on. Close lid; cook for 8 minutes or until the cake springs back when pressed lightly in the centre. Transfer to a wire rack. Turn machine off for 5 minutes to cool slightly. Repeat in batches with remaining cake mixture to make 12 cakes in total.

4 Meanwhile, to make cream cheese topping: Beat cream cheese and butter with electric mixer until light and fluffy. Add icing sugar and lemon rind; beat until smooth.

5 Spread cool hummingbird fingers with cream cheese topping; top with extra toasted coconut and dust with extra cinnamon.

MD APPLE PIES

PREP + COOK TIME 45 MINUTES

⅓ cup (75g) firmly packed brown sugar
1 tablespoon cornflour
1 teaspoon ground cinnamon
800g can apple pie slices, chopped coarsely
2 teaspoons lemon juice
1 teaspoon vanilla bean paste
cooking oil spray
3 sheets frozen butter puff pastry, thawed
40g butter, melted
¼ cup (55g) demerara sugar
icing sugar and vanilla ice-cream, to serve

1 Combine brown sugar, cornflour and cinnamon in a large bowl. Stir in apple slices, lemon juice and vanilla.

2 Spray a 4-hole (2-tablespoon) sausage roll maker with oil.

3 Cut pastry sheets in half. With the machine turned off, position a half pastry sheet to cover the four holes. Press pastry gently into holes. Fill each hole with ¼ cup apple filling. Place another half pastry sheet on top to cover; press around each hole to seal the sides. Brush pies with melted butter; sprinkle each with ½ teaspoon demerara sugar. Using a sharp knife, cut three slits in pastry tops.

4 Turn machine on. Close lid; cook for 10 minutes or until golden and crisp. Transfer to a wire rack. Turn machine off for 5 minutes to cool slightly.

5 Repeat steps 3 and 4 in batches with remaining half pastry sheets, apple filling, melted butter and demerara sugar to make 12 pies in total. Use a sharp knife to cut batches into separate pies.

6 Serve pies dusted with icing sugar and topped with vanilla ice-cream.

COOK'S NOTES
The pastry can be cooked a day ahead. Completed caramel slice can be prepared up to 3 hours ahead and refrigerated until required.

CARAMEL SLICE

PREP + COOK TIME 55 MINUTES (+ REFRIGERATION)

cooking oil spray
2 sheets frozen butter puff pastry, thawed
¾ cup (180ml) milk
½ cup (180g) dulce de leche
100g packet vanilla instant pudding mix
300ml thickened cream
½ cup (80g) icing sugar
2 teaspoons milk, extra

1 Spray a 4-hole (2-tablespoon) sausage roll maker with oil.

2 Cut pastry sheets in half. With the machine turned off, position a half pastry sheet to cover the four holes. Press pastry gently into holes. Turn machine on. Close lid; cook for 12 minutes or until golden. Transfer to a wire rack. Turn machine off for 5 minutes to cool slightly. Repeat in batches with remaining half pastry sheets to make 16 pastry cases in total.

3 Meanwhile, place milk, dulce de leche and pudding mix in the bowl of an electric mixer; mix on low speed until combine. Add cream; beat on medium speed for 2 minutes. Refrigerate for 20 minutes to thicken.

4 Use a sharp knife to cut pastry batches into separate pieces. Stir caramel mixture, then spoon into a piping bag fitted with a 1cm plain nozzle. Pipe caramel over pastry bases, then cover with pastry tops.

5 Combine icing sugar and extra milk in a small bowl. Drizzle over each caramel slice.

GINGER FINGER BUNS WITH FLORENTINE TOPPING

PREP + COOK TIME 50 MINUTES (+ STANDING & COOLING)

2½ cups (375g) plain flour
2 tablespoons caster sugar
2 teaspoons (7g) instant yeast
½ cup (60g) finely chopped crystallised ginger
½ teaspoon finely grated orange rind
1 egg
60g butter, melted
½ cup (125ml) lukewarm milk
cooking oil spray

FLORENTINE TOPPING
60g butter
¼ cup (55g) firmly packed brown sugar
¼ cup (90g) golden syrup
1 cup (80g) flaked almonds, toasted
¾ cup (150g) red glacé cherries, sliced
½ cup (85g) mixed peel

1 Combine flour, sugar, yeast, ginger and orange rind in a large bowl. Whisk egg, butter and milk together in a small jug; add to flour mixture and stir until combined. Knead in the bowl for 2 minutes or until smooth. Cover bowl. Stand in a warm place for 30 minutes or until dough has doubled in size.

2 Turn dough onto a lightly floured surface; gently knead until smooth. Divide dough into 12 even portions; shape each portion into a 10cm log.

3 Spray a 4-hole (2-tablespoon) sausage roll maker with oil.

4 Place four dough logs in holes. Turn machine on. Close lid; cook for 4 minutes. Carefully turn buns over. Close lid; cook for a further 4 minutes or until golden and cooked through. Transfer to a wire rack. Turn machine off for 5 minutes to cool slightly. Repeat cooking in batches with remaining dough logs. Cool completely.

5 Meanwhile, to make florentine topping: Melt butter in a small saucepan over low heat. Add sugar and golden syrup; cook, stirring, for 4 minutes or until sugar dissolves and mixture thickens. Remove from heat; stir in almonds, cherries and mixed peel.

6 Spoon florentine topping on finger buns and leave to cool.

COOK'S NOTES

Store finger buns in an airtight container for up to 2 days. For a flavour variation, use lemon rind instead of orange, and currants instead of crystallised ginger.

MILK CHOCOLATE MOUSSE ÉCLAIRS

PREP + COOK TIME 1 HOUR 10 MINUTES (+ COOLING)

60g butter, chopped
1 tablespoon brown sugar
½ cup (80g) bread flour
3 eggs
cooking oil spray
65g packet Aeroplane creamy chocolate mousse mix
300ml thickened cream

CHOCOLATE TOPPING
⅓ cup (80ml) thickened cream
170g milk chocolate chips
15g butter, chopped
1 tablespoon golden syrup

1 Place butter, sugar and ½ cup (125ml) water in a small saucepan; bring to the boil. Add flour; beat with a wooden spoon over medium heat until mixture comes away from base and side of pan and forms a ball. Cool slightly.

2 Transfer choux pastry to a medium bowl of an electric mixer. Beat in eggs, one at a time, until mixture is smooth and glossy but still holds its shape. Spoon pastry into a piping bag, fitted with a 1.5cm plain nozzle.

3 Spray a 4-hole (2-tablespoon) sausage roll maker with oil.

4 Pipe pastry into 11cm lengths in each hole. Turn machine on. Close lid; cook for 20 minutes or until golden and puffed. Transfer to a wire rack. Turn machine off for 5 minutes to cool slightly. Using a serrated knife, cut éclair cases in half horizontally; remove any soft centres. Return cases to wire rack. Repeat with remaining pastry to make 8 éclairs in total. Cool completely.

5 Whisk chocolate mousse mix and cream in a medium bowl for 2 minutes or until thick and smooth. Spoon chocolate cream into a piping bag fitted with a 5mm plain nozzle. Pipe chocolate cream into éclair bases; position tops on bases.

6 To make chocolate topping: Warm cream in a microwave-safe jug on MEDIUM (50%) for 45 seconds. Add chocolate; whisk until melted and smooth. Whisk in butter and syrup.

7 Spoon chocolate topping on éclairs. Stand on wire rack for 30 minutes or until set.

PORTUGUESE CUSTARD TARTS

PREP + COOK TIME 35 MINUTES (+ COOLING)

1¼ cups (310ml) thick custard
2 egg yolks
½ teaspoon finely grated lemon rind
½ teaspoon vanilla extract
1 tablespoon cornflour
cooking oil spray
1 sheet frozen shortcrust pastry, thawed
2 teaspoons caster sugar

1 Whisk custard, egg yolks, lemon rind, vanilla and cornflour in a medium bowl until combined.

2 Spray a 4-hole (2-tablespoon) sausage roll maker with oil.

3 Cut pastry sheet in half. With machine turned off, position half pastry sheet to cover the four holes. Press pastry gently into holes. Turn machine on. Close lid; cook for 3 minutes. Spoon 2 tablespoons custard filling into each hole. Close lid; cook for a further 8 minutes or until filling is set. Transfer tarts to a wire rack. Turn machine off for 5 minutes to cool.

4 Repeat step 3 with remaining half pastry sheet and custard filling.

5 Sprinkle each tart with ¼ teaspoon sugar; caramelise the top using a kitchen blow torch. Use a sharp knife to cut batches into separate tarts.

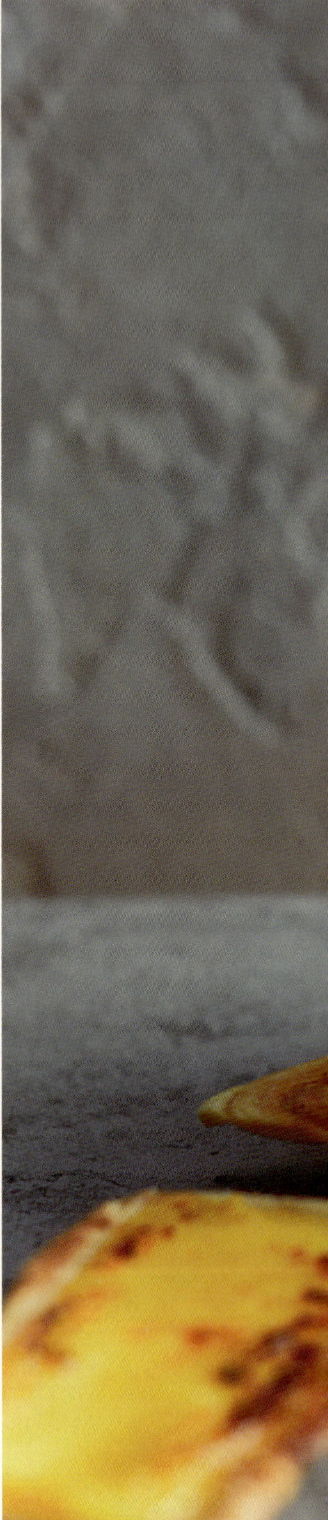

APRICOT & ALMOND TIRAMISU

PREP + COOK TIME 1 HOUR (+ COOLING & REFRIGERATION)

¼ cup (15g) instant coffee granules
1 cup (250ml) boiling water
⅓ cup (80ml) Amaretto liqueur
1 cup (250g) mascarpone
300g ricotta
¼ cup (40g) icing sugar
1 teaspoon vanilla bean paste
4 apricots, stones removed, 2 sliced thinly, 2 sliced thickly
⅓ cup (55g) natural almonds, roasted, chopped coarsely

SPONGE FINGERS
3 eggs
½ cup (110g) caster sugar
1 tablespoon grated lemon rind
½ cup (125ml) vegetable oil
2 cups (300g) self-raising flour
cooking oil spray
2 tablespoons icing sugar
1 tablespoon caster sugar, extra

1 To make the sponge fingers: Beat eggs, caster sugar and lemon rind in a bowl with an electric mixer until thick and creamy. Gradually add vegetable oil in a thin steady stream, beating until combined. Fold in sifted flour, in two batches, until batter is smooth.

2 Spray a 4-hole (2-tablespoon) sausage roll maker with oil. Combine icing sugar and extra caster sugar in a small bowl.

3 Sprinkle ½ teaspoon sugar mixture into the base of each hole. Spoon 2 tablespoons batter into each hole; level surface, spray tops with oil. Sprinkle each top evenly with another ½ teaspoon sugar mixture.

4 Turn machine on. Close lid; cook for 5 minutes. Carefully turn sponge fingers over. Close lid; cook for a further 3 minutes or until golden. Transfer to a wire rack. Turn machine off for 5 minutes to cool slightly.

5 Repeat steps 3 and 4 in batches with more oil spray, remaining sugar mixture and batter to make 14 sponge fingers in total. Cool. Cut sponge fingers in half horizontally.

6 Meanwhile, stir coffee granules, boiling water and liqueur in a heatproof jug; pour into a shallow dish. Cool to room temperature.

7 Beat mascarpone, ricotta, icing sugar and vanilla in a large bowl with electric mixer until firm soft peaks form; do not over whisk. Refrigerate until ready to use.

8 Dip 14 sponge finger halves, one at a time, for a few seconds, into coffee mixture until well covered. Arrange in a single layer in a 2-litre (8-cup) rectangular dish. Top with the thinly sliced apricots; spread with half the mascarpone mixture. Repeat with remaining sponge finger halves, coffee mixture and mascarpone mixture. Cover with plastic wrap; refrigerate overnight.

9 Just before serving, top tiramisu with thickly sliced apricots and chopped almonds.

FIG, TAHINI & SEED BARS

PREP + COOK TIME 40 MINUTES (+ COOLING & STANDING)

2½ cups (85g) rice bubbles
90g soft juicy dried figs
⅓ cup (50g) sunflower seed kernels
¼ cup (50g) pepitas (pumpkin kernel seeds), chopped
½ cup (180g) honey
⅓ cup (90g) hulled tahini
50g butter, melted
⅔ cup (100g) dried apricots, chopped
cooking oil spray
50g white chocolate Melts

1 Place rice bubbles, figs, sunflower seeds, pepitas, honey, tahini, melted butter and half the apricots in a food processor. Pulse until mixture is finely chopped and clumps together.

2 Spray a 4-hole (2-tablespoon) sausage roll maker with oil.

3 Fill each hole with ⅓ cup firmly packed rice bubble mixture. Press mixture firmly and evenly into holes. Press 2 teaspoons of the remaining chopped apricots onto each bar.

4 Turn machine on. Close lid; cook for 4 minutes. Carefully turn bars over using a plastic spatula, reshape if necessary. Close lid; cook for a further 4 minutes until golden brown. Transfer to a wire rack. Turn machine off for 5 minutes to cool slightly.

5 Repeat steps 3 and 4 with more spray oil and remaining rice bubble mixture and chopped apricots to make 8 bars in total. Cool completely.

6 Place chocolate Melts in a microwave-safe bowl. Microwave on MEDIUM (50%), in 20-second bursts, until melted and smooth. Cool slightly.

7 Drizzle melted chocolate over bars; stand for 15 minutes or until chocolate sets.

COOK'S NOTES

This recipe is gluten and nut free. For a flavour variation, use dates instead of figs, craisins instead of apricots and dark chocolate Melts instead of the white.

PEAR & GINGER UPSIDE-DOWN CAKES

PREP + COOK TIME 30 MINUTES (+ COOLING)

450g packet super moist vanilla cupcake mix
2 teaspoons ground ginger
2 eggs
⅓ cup (80ml) milk
60g butter, melted
cooking oil spray
¼ cup (55g) raw sugar
700g jar pears in juice, drained, slices halved
icing sugar, to dust

1 Place cupcake mix, ginger, eggs, milk and butter in a large bowl; stir until just combined.

2 Spray a 4-hole (2-tablespoon) sausage roll maker with oil.

3 Sprinkle 1 teaspoon raw sugar over the base of each hole; top with 2 pieces of pear, then 2 tablespoons cake mixture. Turn machine on. Close lid; cook for 8 minutes or until golden. Transfer to a wire rack to cool completely. Turn machine off for 5 minutes to cool slightly.

4 Repeat step 3 in batches with remaining raw sugar, pear pieces and cake mixture to make 12 cakes in total.

5 Serve upside-down cakes dusted with icing sugar.

***COOK'S NOTES** Save the cupcake cases and icing sachet from the cupcake mix for another use.*

UPSIDE-DOWN CAKE VARIATIONS

MANGO COCONUT

Make Pear & Ginger Upside-down Cakes (recipe page 73), omitting the ginger, replacing the milk with coconut milk and the pear with a canned mango slice (you will need a 695g can mango slices in juice). Cook in batches as directed. Serve cakes topped with toasted coconut flakes.

APPLE, CINNAMON & CRAISIN

Make Pear & Ginger Upside-down Cakes (recipe page 73), replacing ginger with 1 teaspoon ground cinnamon; stir through ¼ cup craisins and replace pear with 2 apple slices (you will need a 770g can apple pie slices). Cook in batches as directed. Serve cakes drizzled with honey.

APRICOT & CARDAMOM

Make Pear & Ginger Upside-down Cakes (recipe page 73), replacing ginger with 1 teaspoon ground cardamom and pear with 2 canned apricot halves (you will need a 695g can apricot halves in juice). Cook in batches as directed. Serve cakes topped with toasted flaked almonds.

LEMON & SALTED COCONUT SLICE

PREP + COOK TIME 45 MINUTES (+ COOLING)

100g butter, softened
⅓ cup (75g) caster sugar
2 eggs
1½ cups (225g) plain flour
cooking oil spray
¼ cup (80g) lemon curd

COCONUT TOPPING
1 egg white
½ cup (110g) caster sugar
2 cups (100g) coconut flakes
½ teaspoon sea salt flakes, crumbled

1 Beat butter and sugar in a small bowl with an electric mixer until light and creamy. Beat in eggs, one at a time, until just combined after each addition. Transfer mixture to a large bowl; stir in sifted flour until a dough forms.

2 To make coconut topping: Whisk egg white in a small bowl with an electric mixer until soft peaks form. Gradually add sugar, beating until sugar has dissolved after each addition and mixture is thick and glossy. Add coconut and salt; use your hands to turn and coat in mixtue.

3 Spray a 4-hole (2-tablespoon) sausage roll maker with oil. Divide dough into 12 portions (each portion will be approximately 1½ tablespoons).

4 With the machine turned off, press four dough portions in holes to create a base. Spread each base evenly with 1 teaspoon lemon curd, then with 1½ tablespoons coconut topping.

5 Close lid; cook for 10 minutes or until topping is golden brown. Turn machine off; leave coconut slice in machine for 5 minutes to cool slightly. Transfer slices to a wire rack to cool completely.

6 Repeat steps 4 and 5 in batches with more oil spray and remaining dough portions, lemon curd and coconut topping to make 12 slices in total. Cool.

RHUBARB & STRAWBERRY CRUMBLE TARTS

PREP + COOK TIME 45 MINUTES (+ COOLING)

240g shortbread biscuits
cooking oil spray
1½ sheets frozen shortcrust pastry, thawed

FRUIT FILLING
½ cup (110g) caster sugar
⅓ cup (80ml) orange juice
500g rhubarb, trimmed, cut into 5cm lengths
2 teaspoons finely grated orange rind
2 teaspoons cornflour
250g strawberries, halved

1 To make fruit filling: Place sugar and orange juice in a medium saucepan; stir over low heat until combined and sugar dissolves. Bring to the boil. Reduce heat. Add rhubarb and orange rind; simmer, covered, for 5 minutes or until rhubarb is tender. Remove from heat; stir in cornflour. Cool. Stir through strawberries.

2 Place shortbread biscuits in a zip-top bag; using a rolling pin, crush into fine crumbs.

3 Spray a 4-hole (2-tablespoon) sausage roll maker with oil.

4 Cut whole pastry sheet in half. With the machine turned off, position a half pastry sheet to cover the four holes. Press pastry gently into holes. Spoon 2 tablespoons fruit filling into each hole, then sprinkle with 1½ tablespoons shortbread crumbs. Close lid; cook for 7 minutes or until shortbread is golden brown. Transfer to a wire rack. Turn machine off for 5 minutes to cool slightly.

5 Repeat step 4 in batches with more spray oil and remaining half pastry sheets, fruit filling and shortbread crumbs to make 12 tarts in total. Use a sharp knife to cut batches into separate tarts.

1
2
3
4
5
6
7

DIY SWEET FILLINGS

With these clever hacks you don't even need a recipe. Fill your chosen pastry with 2-3 tablespoons of your chosen filling, using less if it is runny. Close the lid and cook for 4-8 minutes, flipping the roll halfway through the cooking time. Easy!

1 BERRIES Try fresh (or frozen) strawberries, blueberries or blackberries. Pair them with Nutella or a few pieces of your favourite chocolate bar, or toss with a little sugar and cornflour for berry pie rolls.

2 SPREADS Any spread will work. Try jams, marmalades, passionfruit or lemon curd, Nutella, Biscoff and dulce de leche. These will liquify so pair with something solid such as fruit, crumbled cake, biscuits or marshmallows.

3 RICE PUDDING Use this filling straight up or add a few teaspoons of jam, maramalade, lemon curd or Nutella to the mix. For a fresh fruit spin, add a few berries of your choosing or a little mango.

4 CHOCOLATE BARS Anything and everything is a go with a chocolate bar, really all you need worry about is will it fit and not being too greedy? Some of our favourites are: Reese's peanut butter cups, Lindt chocolate balls (any flavour), Twix bars and rocky road chocolate.

5 CHOCOLATE BISCUITS If you are using uniced chocolate biscuits, chop them up and combine with: Marshmallow fluff, peanut butter, dulce de leche or Nutella. For filled or covered biscuits, amp up the chocolate with a little extra chopped chocolate and choose rectangular bisucits if you want to keep them whole.

6 MARSHMALLOWS For instant s'mores rolls, pair small marshmallows with chunks of chocolate and broken shortbread biscuits.

7 WAFFLES The only thing that will interrupt your D.I.Y manoeuvres is when an ingredient won't fit your machine. Mini waffles can be halved for waffle fingers to fit the machine cavity. Just dust with cinnamon sugar and away you go. Voila! Top with ice-cream for happy mouths.

SOMETHING

SAVOURY

BROCCOLINI & BLUE CHEESE QUICHES

PREP + COOK TIME 35 MINUTES (+ COOLING)

100g broccolini (about ½ bunch)
2 eggs
⅔ cup (160ml) thickened cream
cooking oil spray
1 sheet frozen shortcrust pastry, thawed
80g blue cheese, crumbled
¼ cup (25g) roasted walnuts, chopped

1 Cut broccolini in half lengthways, then cut into 9cm lengths. Bring a medium saucepan of salted water to the boil. Blanch broccolini for 1 minute or until just tender. Drain. Refresh under cold running water.

2 Whisk eggs and cream together in a medium bowl. Season.

3 Spray a 4-hole (2-tablespoon) sausage roll maker with oil.

4 Cut pastry sheet in half. With the machine turned off, position a half pastry sheet to cover the four holes. Press pastry gently into holes. Fill each hole with 1½ tablespoons of egg mixture. Top each with blue cheese and 2 pieces of broccolini.

5 Turn machine on. Close lid; cook for 10 minutes or until pastry is golden and filling is set. Transfer to a wire rack. Turn machine off for 5 minutes to cool slightly.

6 Repeat steps 4 and 5 with more oil spray and remaining half pastry sheet, egg mixture, blue cheese and broccolini to make 8 quiches in total. Use a sharp knife to cut batches into separate quiches.

7 Serve quiches topped with walnuts.

EMPANADAS

PREP + COOK TIME 50 MINUTES (+ COOLING)

1 tablespoon olive oil
1 small onion (80g), chopped finely
¾ cup (80g) frozen diced mixed vegetables
500g beef mince
2 teaspoons ground cumin
2 teaspoons dried oregano
1 teaspoon smoked paprika
½ teaspoon chilli flakes
2 tablespoons pitted kalamata olives, sliced
2 tablespoons tomato paste
¼ cup (60ml) beef stock
cooking oil spray
1 egg yolk
3 sheets frozen puff pastry, thawed
salsa, sour cream and pickled jalapeños, to serve

1 Heat oil in a large non-stick frying pan over a medium high heat; cook onion and mixed vegetables, stirring, for 2 minutes or until vegetables soften. Increase heat to high, add beef; cook, stirring, for 5 minutes or until beef is browned. Add cumin, oregano, paprika and chilli flakes; cook, stirring, for 1 minute or until fragrant. Add olives, tomato paste and stock; cook, stirring, for 1 minute or until stock has evaporated and beef is cooked through. Season to taste. Cool.

2 Spray a 4-hole (2-tablespoon) sausage roll maker with oil. Combine egg yolk with 2 teaspoons cold water in a small bowl for egg wash.

3 Cut pastry sheets in half. With the machine turned off, position a half pastry sheet to cover the four holes. Press pastry gently into holes. Fill each hole with ¼ cup beef mixture. Place a half pastry sheet on top to cover; press around each hole to seal the sides. Brush with egg wash.

4 Turn machine on. Close lid; cook for 6 minutes. Carefully turn rolls over. Close lid; cook for a further 6 minutes or until golden. Transfer to a wire rack. Turn machine off for 5 minutes to cool slightly.

5 Repeat steps 3 and 4 in batches with remaining half pastry sheets, beef mixture and egg wash to make 12 empanadas in total. Use a sharp knife to cut batches into separate rolls.

6 Serve empanadas with salsa, sour cream and pickled jalapeños.

SALMON EN CROÛTE WITH CREAMED SPINACH

PREP + COOK TIME 35 MINUTES (+ COOLING)

4 skinless salmon fillets (460g), halved crossways
2 tablespoons dijon mustard
cooking oil spray
1 egg yolk
2 sheets frozen puff pastry, thawed
lemon wedges, to serve

CREAMED SPINACH
250g frozen chopped spinach, thawed
20g unsalted butter
1 small onion (80g), sliced thinly
1 cup (250ml) thickened cream

1 Toss salmon pieces and dijon mustard together in a medium bowl until coated. Season.

2 Spray a 4-hole (2-tablespoon) sausage roll maker with oil. Combine egg yolk with 2 teaspoons cold water in a small bowl for egg wash.

3 Cut pastry sheets in half. With the machine turned off, position a half pastry sheet to cover the four holes. Press pastry gently into holes. Place one piece of salmon in each hole. Place a half pastry sheet on top to cover; press around each hole to seal the sides. Brush with egg wash.

4 Turn machine on. Close lid; cook for 6 minutes. Carefully turn rolls over. Close lid; cook for a further 6 minutes or until golden. Transfer to a wire rack. Turn machine off for 5 minutes to cool slightly.

5 Repeat steps 3 and 4 with remaining half pastry sheets, salmon pieces and egg wash to make 8 rolls in total. Use a sharp knife to cut batches into separate rolls.

6 Meanwhile, to make creamed spinach: Squeeze excess moisture from spinach. Melt butter in a medium saucepan over medium heat; cook onion, stirring, for 4 minutes or until softened. Add spinach and cream; cook, stirring, for 2 minutes or until thickened slightly. Season to taste.

7 Serve salmon en croûte with creamed spinach and lemon wedges.

SATAY CHICKEN ROLLS

PREP + COOK TIME 35 MINUTES (+ COOLING)

2 teaspoons olive oil
1 small red capsicum (150g), chopped finely
2 cups (320g) shredded cooked chicken breast
1 cup (300g) satay sauce
cooking oil spray
1 egg yolk
2 sheets frozen puff pastry, thawed
cucumber slices, crushed peanuts and lime wedges, to serve

1 Heat oil a large non-stick frying pan over medium-high heat; cook capsicum for 3 minutes or until lightly charred. Cool.

2 Combine chicken, satay sauce and cooled capsicum in a medium bowl. Season to taste.

3 Spray a 4-hole (2-tablespoon) sausage roll maker with oil. Combine egg yolk with 2 teaspoons cold water in a small bowl for egg wash.

4 Cut pastry sheets in half. With the machine turned off, position a half pastry sheet to cover the four holes. Press pastry gently into holes. Fill each hole with ¼ cup chicken mixture. Place a half pastry sheet on top to cover; press around each hole to seal the sides. Brush with egg wash.

5 Turn machine on. Close lid; cook for 6 minutes. Carefully turn rolls over. Close lid; cook for a further 6 minutes or until golden. Transfer to a wire rack. Turn machine off for 5 minutes to cool slightly.

6 Repeat steps 4 and 5 with remaining half pastry sheets, chicken mixture and egg wash to make 8 rolls in total. Use a sharp knife to cut batches into separate rolls.

7 Serve chicken satay rolls with cucumber slices, crushed peanuts and lime wedges.

BEETROOT, GOAT'S CHEESE & THYME TARTS

PREP + COOK TIME 35 MINUTES

25g unsalted butter
1 small red onion (80g), sliced thinly
2 teaspoons thyme leaves, chopped, plus extra to serve
1 clove garlic, crushed
cooking oil spray
1 sheet frozen puff pastry, thawed
200g cooked baby beetroot, sliced thinly
80g soft goat's cheese log, sliced thinly
¼ cup (35g) coarsely chopped roasted hazelnuts (optional)
honey, to serve

1 Melt butter in a small frying pan over medium heat; cook onion, thyme and garlic, stirring, for 5 minutes or until very soft. Season. Cool.

2 Spray a 4-hole (2-tablespoon) sausage roll maker with oil.

3 Cut pastry sheet in half. With the machine turned off, position a half pastry sheet to cover the four holes. Press pastry gently into holes. Add 1 teaspoon of the onion mixture to each hole. Top with alternating slices of beetroot and goat's cheese.

4 Turn machine on. Close lid; cook tarts for 10 minutes or until pastry is golden. Transfer to a wire rack. Turn machine off for 5 minutes to cool slightly.

5 Repeat steps 3 and 4 in batches with more spray oil and the remaining half pastry sheet, onion mixture, beetroot and goat's cheese to make 8 tarts in total. Use a sharp knife to cut batches into separate tarts.

6 Serve tarts topped with hazelnuts and extra thyme leaves; drizzle with honey.

BEEF CURRY PUFFS

PREP + COOK TIME 1 HOUR (+ COOLING)

1 medium potato (200g), peeled, cut into 1cm pieces
1 tablespoon olive oil
1 small red onion (100g), chopped finely
1 small carrot (70g), chopped finely
250g beef mince
¼ cup (30g) frozen peas
1 tablespoon curry powder
1 teaspoon caster sugar
2 tablespoons chopped coriander, plus extra 10 sprigs
cooking oil spray
1 egg yolk
2½ sheets frozen puff pastry, thawed
sweet chilli sauce, to serve

1 Boil potato in a saucepan of salted boiling water for 8 minutes until tender; drain.

2 Meanwhile, heat olive oil in a large frying pan; cook onion and carrot, stirring, for 3 minutes or until vegetables have softened. Add beef; cook, stirring, breaking up with a wooden spoon, for 3 minutes or until browned. Add cooked potato, peas, curry powder and sugar; cook for 1 minute or until fragrant. Add ½ cup (125ml) water; cook, stirring, for 2 minutes or until beef is cooked through and no liquid remains. Season. Cool. Stir through coriander.

3 Spray a 4-hole (2-tablespoon) sausage roll maker with oil. Combine egg yolk with 2 teaspoons cold water in a small bowl for egg wash.

4 Cut whole pastry sheets in half. With the machine turned off, position a half pastry sheet to cover the four holes. Press pastry gently into holes. Fill each hole with ¼ cup of the beef mixture. Place a half pastry sheet on top to cover; press around each hole to seal the sides. Brush with egg wash, then top each roll with an extra coriander sprig.

5 Turn machine on. Close lid; cook for 7 minutes. Carefully turn rolls over. Close lid; cook for a further 7 minutes or until golden. Transfer to a wire rack. Turn machine off for 5 minutes to cool slightly.

6 Repeat steps 4 and 5 with two more half pastry sheets, more beef mixture, egg wash and 4 more coriander sprigs.

7 Cut remaining half pastry sheet crossways in half. Position one pastry piece to cover the two left (front and back) holes. Press pastry gently into holes. Fill with remaining beef mixture. Cover with remaining pastry piece; press around each hole to seal the sides. Brush with egg wash, then top with remaining coriander sprigs. Repeat step 5. Use a sharp knife to cut batches into separate rolls.

8 Serve curry puffs with sweet chilli sauce.

CAMEMBERT FINGERS

PREP + COOK TIME 15 MINUTES

4 sheets fresh fillo pastry
50g unsalted butter, melted
200g camembert wheel, cut into 4 equal slices
2 tablespoons honey
2 teaspoons thyme leaves
apple wedges and thyme sprigs, to serve

1 Lay a sheet of fillo pastry on a work surface. Cover remaining pastry sheets with a damp tea towel to prevent drying out. Brush pastry lightly with melted butter. Top with another sheet of fillo. Brush with more butter. Repeat layering with remaining sheets and more butter. Cut fillo stack into quarters. Place a slice of camembert in the middle of each rectangle. Fold in the short sides; roll up to enclose camembert.

2 Spray a 4-hole (2-tablespoon) sausage roll maker with oil; turn machine on.

3 Place camembert fingers, seam-side down, in holes; brush tops with melted butter. Close lid; cook for 4 minutes. Carefully turn fingers over. Close lid; cook for a further 4 minutes or until golden. Transfer to a wire rack.

4 Meanwhile, combine honey and thyme in a microwave-safe jug. Microwave on MEDIUM (50%) for 20 seconds or until warmed through.

5 Serve camembert fingers with honey mixture, apple wedges and thyme sprigs.

COOK'S NOTES We used fresh fillo pastry found in the refrigerated section of supermarkets. Each sheet measures 28cm x 40cm.

COOK'S NOTES

For vegan sausage rolls, use a plant-based cheese and omit using the egg wash. Serve with tomato or chilli sauce. Rolls can be frozen for up to 1 month.

VEGIE SAUSAGE ROLLS

PREP + COOK TIME 35 MINUTES (+ COOLING)

6 vegetarian sausages (350g)
1 small carrot (70g), grated finely
½ cup (60g) coarsely grated sharp cheddar cheese
1 tsp Vegemite
1 teaspoon fresh thyme leaves
1 teaspoon chilli flakes (optional)
cooking oil spray
1 egg yolk
2 sheets frozen puff pastry, thawed
2 tablespoons poppy seeds
sauce of your choice, to serve

1 If the sausage has a casing, cut a slit at the end of each sausage and squeeze out sausage filling. If the sausage doesn't have a casing, crumble it into a bowl. Add carrot, cheese, Vegemite, thyme and chilli flakes. Using your hands, mix until well combined. Season.

2 Spray a 4-hole (2-tablespoon) sausage roll maker with oil. Combine egg yolk with 2 teaspoons cold water in a small bowl for egg wash.

3 Cut pastry sheets in half. With the machine turned off, position a half pastry sheet to cover the four holes. Press pastry gently into holes. Fill each hole with ¼ cup of the sausage mixture. Place a half pastry sheet on top to cover; press around each hole to seal the sides. Brush with egg wash. Sprinkle with poppy seeds.

4 Turn machine on. Close lid; cook for 6 minutes. Carefully turn rolls over. Close lid; cook for a further 6 minutes or until golden. Transfer to a wire rack. Turn machine off for 5 minutes to cool slightly.

5 Repeat steps 3 and 4 with remaining half pastry sheets, sausage mixture and egg wash to make 8 rolls in total. Use a sharp knife to cut batches into separate rolls.

6 Serve sausage rolls with sauce.

REUBEN WRAPS

PREP + COOK TIME 25 MINUTES (+ COOLING)

8 x 25cm wholegrain wraps
⅓ cup (80ml) thousand island dressing, plus extra to serve
16 pastrami slices (210g)
8 swiss cheese slices (160g)
½ cup (75g) sauerkraut
cooking oil spray
bread and butter pickles and crinkle-cut potato chips, to serve

1 Heat wraps according to packet instructions.

2 Place a wrap on a work surface. Cut a 4cm strip lengthways from both edges of the wrap. Spread 1 teaspoon of dressing on the wrap. Place 2 slices pastrami and 1 slice cheese in the centre of each wrap; top with 1 tablespoon sauerkraut. Fold in the cut sides of the wrap. Roll from the bottom edge to enclose the filling. Repeat filling and rolling with remaining wraps, dressing, pastrami, cheese and sauerkraut to make 8 wraps in total.

3 Spray a 4-hole (2-tablespoon) sausage roll maker with oil.

4 Place four rolled wraps in holes, spray with oil. Turn machine on. Close lid; cook for 4 minutes. Turn rolls over. Close lid; cook for a further 4 minutes or until golden. Transfer to a tray, cover to keep warm. Turn machine off for 5 minutes to cool slightly. Repeat with remaining rolled wraps.

5 Serve reuben wraps with pickles, potato chips and extra dressing.

COOK'S NOTES
Buttering inside the rolls keeps them from getting soggy.
Yakisoba sauce is available in the Asian aisle of supermarkets or from Asian grocers.

YAKISOBA PAN

PREP + COOK TIME 15 MINUTES

85g packet instant mi goreng noodles
1 tablespoon yakisoba sauce
2 teaspoons vegetable oil
1½ cups (120g) slaw mix
4 brioche hot dog rolls (200g)
40g salted butter, at room temperature
cooking oil spray
red pickled ginger, nori flakes and japanese mayonnaise, to serve

1 Cook noodles according to packet directions. Drain. Stir in seasoning packets and yakisoba sauce.

2 Meanwhile, heat vegetable oil in a medium frying pan over medium-high heat; cook slaw for 1 minute or until just softened. Remove pan from heat; stir in noodles to combine. Season to taste.

3 Split rolls vertically from the top without cutting all the way through. Carefully spread butter on the inside of each roll. Using tongs place ¼ cup of noodle mixture in each roll.

4 Spray a 4-hole (2-tablespoon) sausage roll maker with oil.

5 Place two filled rolls diagonally over the holes. Turn machine on. Place a wooden spoon across the front of the machine then gently lower the lid (the lid will not quite touch the top of the rolls). Cook for 5 minutes or until rolls are golden brown. Transfer to a serving plate. Turn machine off for 5 minutes to cool slightly. Repeat with remaining filled rolls.

6 Serve yakisoba rolls topped with pickled ginger and nori flakes; drizzle with japanese mayonnaise.

TOAD IN THE 'ROLL'

PREP + COOK TIME 35 MINUTES

cooking oil spray
8 chipolata sausages (200g)
2 eggs
¾ cup (180ml) milk
1 cup (150g) plain flour
tomato sauce and peas, to serve

ONION GRAVY
30g butter
1 medium onion (150g), sliced thinly
2 thyme sprigs
250g pouch liquid gravy

1 Spray a 4-hole (2-tablespoon) sausage roll maker with oil; turn machine on. Place 4 sausages in holes. Close lid. Cook for 6 minutes, turning halfway or until cooked through. Transfer to a plate. Turn machine off for 5 minutes to cool slightly. Repeat cooking with remaining sausages. Leave machine on.

2 Meanwhile, whisk eggs and milk in a jug. Place flour and ½ teaspoon salt in a medium bowl. Slowly pour egg mixture into flour mixture, whisking continuously, until smooth.

3 Spray holes generously with oil. Pour ¼ cup of the batter into each hole. Place a cooked sausage in the centre of each hole. Close the lid; cook for 8 minutes or until golden. Transfer to a plate; cover to keep warm. Repeat with remaining batter and sausages to make 8 in total.

4 Meanwhile, make the onion gravy: Melt butter in a medium saucepan over medium heat; cook onion and thyme, stirring, for 6 minutes or until softened. Pour in gravy, stir to combine. Cook for 1 minute or until heated through. Season. Discard thyme.

5 Serve toad in the rolls as soon as possible, topped with tomato sauce and gravy, and with peas.

COOK'S NOTES

Based on Yorkshire puddings, this recipe works best with a preheated machine to help the batter puff up. Make sure to eat these rolls before they deflate.

MAKES MAKES MAKES MAKES 8

VEGETARIAN INDIAN-STYLE KATHI ROLLS

PREP + COOK TIME 30 MINUTES

25g ghee or butter
200g paneer, cut into 1cm pieces
½ cup (80g) frozen chopped spinach, thawed
400g can chickpeas, drained, rinsed
¾ cup (200g) tikka masala simmer sauce
8 round roti wraps
cooking oil spray
mint leaves, extra, to serve

CUCUMBER RAITA
1 medium lebanese cucumber (130g), grated
1 cup (280g) greek yoghurt
½ teaspoon ground cumin
2 teaspoons lemon juice
1 tablespoon sliced mint leaves

1 Heat ghee in a large frying pan over a medium-high heat; cook paneer for 3 minutes or until golden.

2 Squeeze any excess moisture from spinach; add to frying pan with the chickpeas and simmer sauce. Cook for 2 minutes or until heated through. Remove pan from heat. Season. Cool slightly.

3 Heat roti wraps according to packet directions.

4 Place a heated wrap on a work surface. Spoon ¼ cup of the filling mixture in the centre of the wrap in a 10cm log shape. Fold the bottom edge of the wrap over the filling; roll over once. Fold in the sides, then continue rolling to enclose the filling. Repeat with remaining wraps and filling to make 8 kathi rolls in total.

5 Place four kathi rolls in holes of a 4-hole (2-tablespoon) sausage roll maker. Spray tops with oil. Turn machine on. Close lid; cook for 5 minutes or until golden. Transfer to a tray; cover to keep warm. Turn machine off for 5 minutes to cool slightly. Repeat with remaining kathi rolls.

6 To make cucumber raita, combine ingredients in a medium bowl. Season to taste.

7 Serve kathi rolls warm with cucumber raita and extra mint leaves.

OKONOMIYAKI ROLLS

PREP + COOK TIME 25 MINUTES

⅔ cup (100g) plain flour
½ teaspoon baking powder
1 egg, beaten lightly
2 teaspoons soy sauce
1 teaspoon sesame oil
1½ cups (120g) slaw mix
1 clove garlic, crushed
2 teaspoons finely grated ginger
cooking oil spray
tonkatsu sauce, japanese mayonnaise, finely chopped green onion and crisp fried onions, to serve

QUICK PICKLED CUCUMBER

2 tablespoons rice wine or white wine vinegar
2 teaspoons caster sugar
¼ teaspoon fine salt
1 medium lebanese cucumber (130g), peeled into ribbons

1 To make quick pickled cucumber: Combine vinegar, sugar, salt and 2 tablespoons water in a medium bowl until sugar dissolves. Add cucumber. Set aside, tossing occasionally.

2 Meanwhile, place flour and baking powder in a medium bowl. Combine egg, soy sauce, sesame oil and ⅓ cup (80ml) water in a jug. Slowly pour egg mixture into flour mixture, whisking continuously until smooth. Add slaw mix, garlic and ginger; stir to combine.

3 Spray a 4-hole (2-tablespoon) sausage roll maker with oil.

4 Fill each hole with ¼ cup of the mixture. Turn machine on. Close lid; cook for 7 minutes. Carefully turn rolls over. Close lid; cook for a further 7 minutes or until golden. Turn machine off. Leave rolls in machine for 1 minute.

5 Drain pickled cucumber. Drizzle rolls with tonkatsu sauce and mayonnaise; sprinkle with green onion and crisp fried onions. Serve with pickled cucumber.

COOK'S NOTES

Tonkatsu sauce, japanese mayonnaise and crispy fried onions can be found in the Asian aisle of supermarkets or at Asian grocers.

KIMCHI & CHEESE ROLLS

PREP + COOK TIME 15 MINUTES

1 egg, beaten lightly
1 tablespoon kimchi brine
½ cup (75g) plain flour
1 tablespoon cornflour
1 cup (200g) drained kimchi, chopped
¾ cup (80g) grated tasty cheese
cooking oil spray
1 tablespoon toasted sesame seeds
1 green onion, sliced thinly

DIPPING SAUCE

¼ cup soy sauce
3 teaspoons rice wine vinegar
1½ teaspoons caster sugar

1 Combine egg, kimchi brine and ¼ cup (60ml) water in a jug. Place flours in a medium bowl. Slowly pour the egg mixture into the flour mixture, whisking continuously until smooth. Stir through kimchi and ½ cup of the cheese. Season.

2 Spray a 4-hole (2-tablespoon) sausage roll maker with oil.

3 Fill each hole with ¼ cup of the mixture. Sprinkle with sesame seeds and remaining cheese. Turn the machine on. Close lid; cook for 8 minutes or until puffed and golden. Turn machine off. Lift the lid; leave rolls in machine for 1 minute.

4 Meanwhile, to make dipping sauce, combine ingredients with 1 tablespoon water in a small bowl.

5 Serve rolls topped with green onion and with dipping sauce.

***COOK'S NOTES** You could easily make a double batch of these tasty rolls.*

MOZZARELLA STICKS

PREP + COOK TIME 30 MINUTES (+ COOLING)

2 eggs
1½ cups (110g) panko (japanese) breadcrumbs
½ cup (40g) finely grated parmesan
2 tablespoons finely chopped flat-leaf parsley
2 x 256g blocks mozzarella
olive oil cooking spray
spicy tomato relish, to serve

1 Whisk eggs in a shallow bowl. Combine breadcrumbs, parmesan and parsley in a second shallow bowl.

2 Cut each mozzarella block into four 2cm x 9cm sticks. Working with one mozzarella stick at a time at a time, dip sticks in egg, then coat in breadcrumb mixture. Repeat dipping and coating so all sticks are double coated.

3 Spray a 4-hole (2-tablespoon) sausage roll maker with oil; turn machine on.

4 Place four double-coated mozzarella sticks in holes; spray with oil. Close lid; cook for 8 minutes or until golden. Transfer to a tray; cover to keep warm. Turn machine off for 5 minutes to cool slightly. Repeat with remaining double-coated mozzarella sticks.

5 Serve mozzarella sticks with spicy tomato relish.

MAKES 8

HALOUMI & FALAFEL TURKISH WRAPS

PREP + COOK TIME 30 MINUTES

1 tablespoon olive oil
180g haloumi, cut lengthways into 8 slices
4 x 27.5cm lebanese flatbreads (500g)
⅓ cup (80ml) garlic kebab sauce
2 tablespoons hot chilli sauce
¼ cup flat-leaf parsley leaves
12 pre-made falafels (225g)
cooking oil spray
hummus and lemon wedges, to serve

TURKISH SALAD
1 medium lebanese cucumber (130g), seeded, sliced thinly
200g cherry tomatoes, quartered
½ small red onion (40g), sliced thinly
1 tablespoon extra virgin olive oil
2 teaspoons lemon juice

1 Heat olive oil in a large frying pan over a medium-high heat; cook haloumi for 2 minutes on each side or until golden. Set aside.

2 Meanwhile, heat a flatbread on MEDIUM (50%) power for 15 seconds in a microwave. Cut wrap in half to create 2 semi-circles.

3 Place a halved wrap on a work surface. Spread 2 teaspoons of garlic kebab sauce and 1 teaspoon hot chilli sauce in the centre of the wrap; top with parsley. Place a slice of haloumi in the centre. Crumble 1½ falafels over the haloumi. Fold the flat edge of the wrap over the filling, roll over once. Fold in the sides, then continue to roll to enclose the filling.

4 Repeat steps 2 and 3 with remaining wraps, filling ingredients and haloumi to make 8 wraps in total.

5 Spray a 4-hole (2-tablespoon) sausage roll maker with oil.

6 Place four filled wraps in holes; spray tops with oil. Turn machine on. Close lid; cook for 5 minutes or until golden. Transfer to a tray; cover to keep warm. Turn machine off for 5 minutes to cool slightly. Repeat with remaining filled wraps.

7 To make turkish salad, combine ingredients in a bowl. Season to taste.

8 Serve turkish wraps with salad, hummus and lemon wedges.

MEXICAN RICE-STUFFED MINI CAPSICUMS

PREP + COOK TIME 20 MINUTES

250g packet microwave Mexican-style rice
½ cup (60g) grated mexican cheese blend
¼ cup coarsely chopped coriander leaves, plus extra to serve
8 sweet mini vine capsicums (55g each)
cooking oil spray
sour cream and extra virgin olive oil, to serve

1 Heat rice according to packet directions.

2 Combine rice, cheese and coriander in a medium bowl; season.

3 Using a sharp knife, make a cut down one side of each capsicum; remove the seeds and membrane. Spoon 2 tablespoons of the filling into each capsicum.

4 Spray a 4-hole (2-tablespoon) sausage roll maker with oil.

5 Place four filled capsicums in holes cut-side facing sideways; spray tops with oil. Turn machine on. Close lid; cook for 5 minutes until golden. Transfer to a tray; cover to keep warm. Wipe machine clean with paper towel. Turn machine off for 5 minutes to cool slightly. Repeat with remaining filled capsicums.

6 Serve stuffed capsicums with sour cream, drizzled with olive oil and extra coriander.

COOK'S NOTES

You need a packet of 24 (500g) mini lotus leaf buns from Asian grocers. Lotus buns are similar to many bao buns and are identified by their folded shape.

PORK BUNS

PREP + COOK TIME 30 MINUTES (+ COOLING)

300g pork mince
2 cloves garlic, crushed
4 green onions, chopped finely, plus extra to serve
2 tablespoons char siu sauce
⅓ cup finely chopped coriander leaves, plus extra leaves to serve
16 mini lotus leaf buns, thawed (22g each)
cooking oil spray
sweet chilli sauce, to serve

1 Combine pork, garlic, green onion, char siu sauce and coriander in a medium bowl.

2 Reheat lotus leaf buns according to packet directions in the microwave.

3 Shape 1 tablespoon of pork mixture into sausage shapes to fit the buns, and making 16 in total. Fill buns with shaped pork mixture.

4 Spray a 4-hole (2-tablespoon) sausage roll maker with oil.

5 Place four filled buns in holes. Turn machine on. Close lid; cook for 5 minutes or until buns are golden brown and filling is cooked. Transfer to a tray; cover to keep warm. Turn machine off for 5 minutes to cool slightly. Repeat in batches with remaining filled buns (repeat batches may cook a little faster each time).

6 Serve buns with extra green onion, extra coriander leaves and sweet chilli sauce.

PORK & APPLE SAUSAGE ROLLS

PREP + COOK TIME 30 MINUTES

2 small baby green apples (200g)
500g pork mince
½ cup (40g) finely grated parmesan
1 tablespoon dijon mustard
1 tablespoon thyme leaves, plus 16 sprigs extra
2 eggs, beaten lightly
olive oil cooking spray
2 sheets frozen puff pastry, thawed
apple sauce, to serve

1 Core apples; cut in half. Dice 1 apple half; cut remaining halves into 2mm thin wedges to get 24 slices in total. Combine pork, diced apple, parmesan, mustard, thyme and egg in a medium bowl; season.

2 Spray a 4-hole (2-tablespoon) sausage roll maker with oil.

3 Cut pastry sheets in half. With the machine turned off, position a half pastry sheet to cover the four holes. Press pastry gently into holes. Fill each hole with ¼ cup of the pork mixture. Place another half sheet on top to cover; press around each hole to seal the sides. Spray with oil then top each roll with 3 slices of apple and 2 of the extra thyme sprigs.

4 Turn machine on. Close lid; cook for 12 minutes or until golden. Transfer to a wire rack. Turn machine off for 5 minutes to cool.

5 Repeat steps 3 and 4 with more oil spray and the remaining half pastry sheets, pork mixture, apple slices and extra thyme sprigs. Use a sharp knife to cut batches into separate rolls.

SALT & PEPPER TOFU BÁNH MÌ

PREP + COOK TIME 45 MINUTES

1½ tablespoons sesame oil
2 tablespoons sesame seeds
2 tablespoons black sesame seeds
½ teaspoon chinese five spice powder
2 teaspoons sea salt flakes
¼ teaspoon ground white pepper
450g firm tofu, drained, pat dry
olive oil cooking spray
8 brioche hot dog rolls (400g)
2 green onions, cut into lengths, then thin strips
1 medium carrot (120g), julienned
1 long red chilli, sliced thinly, plus extra to serve
japanese mayonnaise, small coriander leaves and soy sauce, to serve

1 Place sesame oil in a shallow bowl. Combine sesame seeds, five spice powder, salt and pepper in another shallow bowl.

2 Cut tofu into eight 3cm x 8.5cm rectangular pieces. Working with one piece at a time, dip tofu in sesame oil then coat in sesame seed mixture.

3 Spray a 4-hole (2-tablespoon) sausage roll maker with oil.

4 Place four salt and pepper coated pieces of tofu in holes; spray tops with oil. Turn machine on. Close lid; cook for 8 minutes. Carefully turn tofu over. Close lid; cook for a further 8 minutes or until golden. Transfer to a tray, cover to keep warm. Turn machine off for 5 minutes to cool slightly. Repeat with remaining salt and pepper tofu. Cut tofu in half lengthways on the diagonal.

5 To serve, split brioche rolls vertically from the top without cutting all the way through; spread inside with mayonnaise. Fill rolls with green onion, carrot, salt and pepper tofu, coriander leaves and chilli. Serve bánh mì with soy sauce topped with extra sliced chilli.

PESTO SCROLLS

PREP + COOK TIME 35 MINUTES

250g fresh pizza dough, at room temperature
½ cup (130g) basil pesto
⅔ cup (100g) finely chopped barbecue chicken
⅔ cup (70g) grated pizza cheese
basil leaves, to serve

1 Turn dough out onto a lightly floured surface; cut into four even portions. Roll each portion into a 12cm x 18cm rectangle.

2 Spread the base of one dough rectangle with 1½ tablespoons pesto, leaving a 2cm border. Spoon 2 tablespoons each of chicken and pizza cheese over the pesto. From the long edge, fold bottom of dough over filling then continue rolling to enclose filling. Cut roll into six 3cm piece. Repeat with remaining dough portions, pesto, chicken and cheese to make 24 scrolls in total.

3 Spray a 4-hole (2-tablespoon) sausage roll maker with oil; turn machine on.

4 Place three scrolls, cut-side up, in each hole. Close lid; cook for 10 minutes or until dough is puffed and golden. Transfer to a tray; cover keep warm. Turn machine off for 5 minutes to cool. Repeat with remaining pesto scrolls.

5 Serve pesto scrolls topped with basil leaves.

FALAFELS

PREP + COOK TIME 35 MINUTES

400g can chickpeas, drained, rinsed
1 clove garlic, crushed
2 green onions, chopped coarsely
¼ cup flat-leaf parsley leaves, chopped finely
⅓ cup (50g) plain flour
½ teaspoon baking powder
1 teaspoon ground cumin
1 egg
olive oil cooking spray
4 greek pitta bread, grilled
baby cos leaves, hummus and pickled turnips, to serve

1 Process chickpeas, garlic, green onion, parsley, flour, baking powder, cumin and egg until mixture just comes together; season. Shape 1 heaped tablespoon of chickpea mixture to make 16 falafels in total.

2 Spray a 4-hole (2-tablespoon) sausage roll maker with oil.

3 Place two falafels in each hole; spray tops with oil. Turn machine on. Close lid; cook for 5 minutes. Carefully turn falafels over. Close lid; cook for a further 5 minutes or until golden. Transfer to a tray; cover to keep warm. Turn machine off for 5 minutes to cool slightly. Repeat with remaining falafels.

4 Serve falafels on greek pitta bread with lettuce, hummus and pickled turnips.

CHICKEN KIEV ROLLS

PREP + COOK TIME 30 MINUTES

160g butter, softened
⅓ cup finely chopped flat-leaf parsley, plus 16 leaves extra
2 cloves garlic, crushed
2 teaspoons finely grated lemon rind
2 tablespoons panko (japanese) breadcrumbs
8 chicken tenderloins (480g)
cooking oil spray
1 egg yolk
2 sheets frozen puff pastry, thawed
salad leaves, to serve

1 Combine butter, chopped parsley, garlic, lemon rind and breadcrumbs in a small bowl.

2 Using a sharp knife make a cut three-quarters of the way through the sides of the chicken. Spoon 2 teaspoons butter mixture into the cavity, closing over to seal.

3 Spray a 4-hole (2-tablespoon) sausage roll maker with oil. Combine egg yolk and 2 teaspoons water in a small bowl for egg wash.

4 Cut pastry sheets in half. With the machine turned off, position a half pastry sheet to cover the four holes. Fill each hole with a filled chicken tenderloin. Place a half pastry sheet on top to cover; press around each hole to seal the sides. Brush rolls with egg wash, then top each roll with 2 of the extra parsley leaves.

5 Turn machine on. Close lid; cook for 10 minutes or until golden. Transfer to a tray; cover to keep warm. Turn machine off for 5 minutes to cool slightly.

6 Repeat steps 4 and 5 with remaining half pastry sheets, filled chicken tenderloins, egg wash and extra parsley leaves. Use a sharp knife to cut batches into separate rolls.

7 Serve chicken kiev rolls with salad leaves.

MAKES MAKES MAKES MAKES 6

FISH CROQUETTES

PREP + COOK TIME 30 MINUTES

3 eggs

½ x 475g tub bought mashed potato

¼ cup (35g) sage and onion breadcrumb stuffing

2 teaspoons finely grated lemon rind

4 green onions, chopped finely

1 cup (100g) grated pizza cheese

2 teaspoons dijon mustard

2 tablespoons chopped dill

200g hot-smoked salmon, flaked

¾ cup (75g) panko (japanese) breadcrumbs

cooking oil spray

crème fraîche, extra dill and lemon cheeks, to serve

1 Beat 1 egg in a medium bowl. Add mashed potato, sage and onion stuffing, lemon rind, green onion, pizza cheese, mustard, dill and flaked salmon; season with salt and pepper. Mix until well combined. Shape ⅓ cup of the mixture into six 9cm logs.

2 Beat remaining 2 eggs in a shallow bowl. Place breadcrumbs in a second shallow bowl. Working with one at a time, dip croquettes in egg, then coat in breadcrumbs.

3 Spray a 4-hole (2-tablespoon) sausage roll maker with oil.

4 Place four croquettes in holes. Turn machine on. Close lid; cook for 8 minutes or until golden brown and firm. Transfer to a baking-paper-lined tray; cover to keep warm. Turn machine off for 5 minutes to cool slightly. Repeat with remaining croquettes.

5 Serve croquettes with crème fraîche, extra dill and lemon cheeks.

FRIED RICE ROLLS

PREP + COOK TIME 30 MINUTES

250g packet microwave special fried rice

80g sliced chinese barbecue pork, chopped finely

⅓ cup (40g) frozen peas

2 green onions, sliced thinly, plus extra to serve

3 teaspoons nasi goreng rice paste

¼ cup finely chopped fresh coriander, plus extra to serve

2 eggs, beaten lightly

cooking oil spray

soy sauce, to serve

1 Heat rice according to packet directions.

2 Combine rice, barbecued pork, peas, green onion, paste, coriander and egg in a medium bowl; season.

3 Spray a 4-hole (2-tablespoon) sausage roll maker with oil.

4 Fill each hole with ¼ cup of the rice mixture. Turn machine on. Close lid; cook for 6 minutes. Carefully turn over. Close lid; cook for a further 6 minutes or until golden. Transfer to a tray; cover to keep warm. Turn machine off for 5 minutes to cool slightly.

5 Repeat step 4 with more oil and the remaining rice mixture to make 8 rolls in total.

6 Serve fried rice rolls topped with extra finely chopped green onion and coriander, and with soy sauce.

ZUCCHINI & PASTA FRITTER ROLLS

PREP + COOK TIME 40 MINUTES (+ COOLING)

300g packet quick macaroni
3 medium zucchini (360g)
1 cup (80g) finely grated parmesan
2 tablespoons finely chopped flat-leaf parsley
2 green onions, sliced thinly
1 clove garlic, crushed
¼ cup (35g) plain flour
2 eggs, beaten lightly
olive oil cooking spray
crème fraîche, rocket leaves and lemon wedges, to serve

1 Heat pasta according to packet directions. Coarsely grate zucchini, place in a sieve; squeeze out excess moisture, drain well.

2 Combine pasta, zucchini, ¾ cup of the parmesan, the parsley, green onion, garlic, flour and egg in a medium bowl; season.

3 Spray a 4-hole (2-tablespoon) sausage roll maker with oil.

4 Fill each hole with ¼ cup of zucchini mixture. Turn machine on. Close lid; cook for 8 minutes. Carefully turn fritters over. Close lid; cook for a further 2 minutes or until golden. Transfer to a tray; cover to keep warm. Turn machine off for 5 minutes to cool slightly. Repeat in batches with remaining zucchini mixture to make 12 fritter rolls in total.

5 Serve fritter rolls with crème fraîche, rocket leaves and lemon wedges.

EGGPLANT ROLLS

PREP + COOK TIME 35 MINUTES

1 eggplant (400g) (17cm long)
200g firm ricotta
2 tablespoons finely chopped flat-leaf parsley
1 clove garlic, crushed
¾ cup (60g) finely grated parmesan, plus extra to serve
1 egg, beaten lightly
¼ cup (20g) panko (japanese) breadcrumbs
cooking oil spray
1 cup (260g) bottled tomato pasta sauce
flat-leaf parsley sprigs, to serve

1 Trim the stem from the eggplant. Cut eggplant lengthways into 3mm thin slices. You need 8 slices, each one should be 8.5cm x 14cm.

2 Combine ricotta, parsley, garlic, parmesan, egg and breadcrumbs in a medium bowl; season.

3 Working with one at a time, place eggplant slices on a work surface, with the short side in front of you. Spray both sides well with oil. Place 2 tablespoons ricotta mixture along the base of the short side; roll up to enclose the filling.

4 Spray a 4-hole (2-tablespoon) sausage roll maker with oil.

5 Place four eggplant rolls, seam-side down, in holes. Turn machine on. Close lid; cook for 10 minutes or until golden. Transfer to a tray; cover to keep warm. Turn machine off for 5 minutes to cool slightly. Repeat with remaining eggplant rolls.

6 Place pasta sauce in a microwave-safe bowl. Microwave on HIGH (100%), in 30-second bursts, until heated through.

7 Serve eggplant rolls topped with tomato sauce, extra grated parmesan and parsley sprigs.

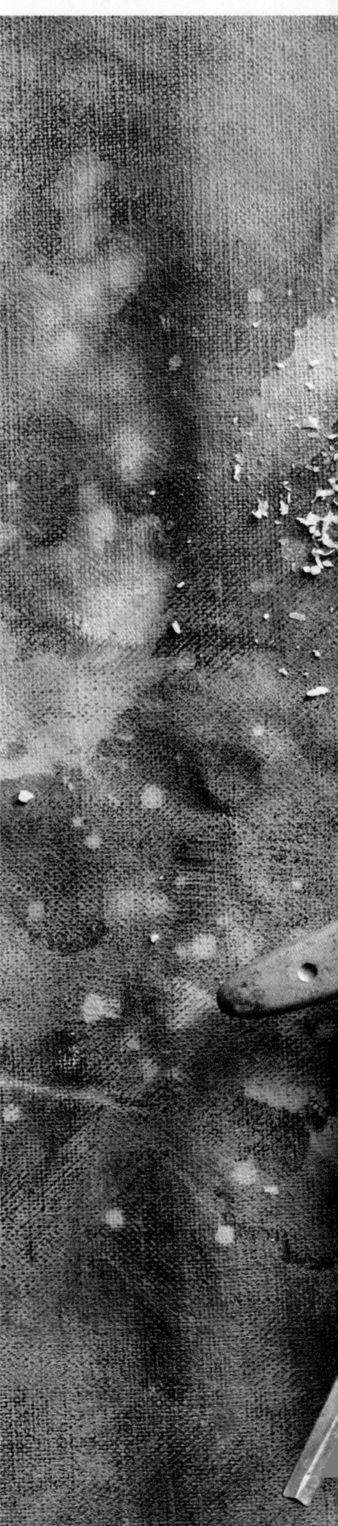

YAKITORI SALMON

PREP + COOK TIME 20 MINUTES (+ REFRIGERATION)

700g skinless centre-cut salmon fillets
½ cup (125ml) yakitori sauce
olive oil cooking spray
8 x 15cm wooden skewers
2 green onions, chopped finely
1 tablespoon sesame seeds, toasted
steamed rice and edamame, to serve

1 Cut salmon into 24 x 3cm cubes. Place salmon in a medium bowl with yakitori sauce; toss to coat well. Cover; refrigerate for 10 minutes.

2 Drain salmon, reserving the marinade. Spray a 4-hole (2-tablespoon) sausage roll maker with oil.

3 Fill each hole with 3 cubes of salmon. Turn machine on. Close lid; cook for 5 minutes or until golden and cooked through but still pink in the centre. Thread 3 salmon cubes each onto 4 skewers. Transfer to a tray, cover to keep warm. Repeat with remaining salmon cubes and skewers to make 8 skewers in total (the second batch of skewers will cook slightly faster than the first).

4 Meanwhile, place reserved marinade in a small saucepan; bring to the boil. Reduce heat; simmer for 3 minutes or until sauce has reduced and thickened slightly.

5 Top salmon skewers with sauce, green onion and sesame seeds. Serve with steamed rice and edamame.

***COOK'S NOTES** If you prefer, you can thread the salmon cubes onto 10cm wooden skewers before cooking in the machine. If you do, soak the skewers first in boiling water for 10 minutes.*

TURKISH CIGARS

PREP + COOK TIME 35 MINUTES

125g haloumi, grated coarsely
125g fetta, crumbled
½ cup (60g) grated cheddar
¼ teaspoon ground allspice
¼ cup finely chopped fresh mint
8 sheets fillo pastry
100g butter, melted
cooking oil spray
1 tablespoon nigella seeds
pomegranate molasses and small fresh mint leaves, to serve

1 Combine cheeses, allspice and chopped mint in a medium bowl; season.

2 Lay a sheet of fillo pastry on a work surface. Cover remaining sheets with a damp tea towel to prevent drying out. Brush pastry lightly with the melted butter. Fold in half lengthways; brush with more butter. Fold in half crossways to form a 14cm x 22cm rectangle.

3 Spoon 2 tablespoons cheese filling along one short edge of the pastry, leaving a 1cm border; roll up tightly, folding in the sides as you roll. Repeat with remaining pastry sheets, more butter and cheese mixture to make 8 cigars in total.

4 Spray a 4-hole (2-tablespoon) sausage roll maker with oil; turn machine on.

5 Place four cigars, seam-side down, in holes; brush tops with more melted butter. Sprinkle each with ⅛ teaspoon nigella seeds. Close lid; cook for 5 minutes. Carefully turn cigars over. Close lid; cook for a further 5 minutes or until golden. Transfer to a wire rack, cover to keep warm. Turn machine off for 5 minutes to cool slightly. Repeat with remaining cigars, melted butter and nigella seeds.

6 Serve cigars with pomegranate molasses and mint leaves.

HASH BROWNS

PREP + COOK TIME 20 MINUTES

500g desiree potatoes, peeled
2 eggs, beaten lightly
2 teaspoons finely chopped thyme
50g butter, melted, cooled slightly
olive oil cooking spray
20g butter, softened, extra
tomato sauce, pan-fried streaky bacon, tomato halves and mushrooms, to serve

1 Coarsely grate potatoes. Squeeze out as much liquid as possible in a clean tea towel. Place grated potato in a bowl with the egg, thyme and melted butter; season well with salt and pepper. Stir to combine.

2 Spray a 4-hole (2-tablespoon) sausage roll maker with oil.

3 Fill each hole with ⅓ cup potato mixture. Dot tops with the extra butter. Turn machine on. Close lid; cook for 10 minutes. Turn hash browns over. Close lid; cook for a further 5 minutes or until hash browns are golden brown and firm.

4 Serve hash browns with tomato sauce, bacon, tomatoes and mushrooms.

***COOK'S NOTES** If you like, you can cook the bacon, tomato halves and mushrooms in the sausage roll maker. Cook bacon for 8 minutes; tomato halves and mushrooms for 6 minutes.*

BREAKFAST TARTS

PREP + COOK TIME 30 MINUTES

cooking oil spray
1 sheet frozen puff pastry, thawed
8 round slices leg ham (80g)
8 extra-large eggs (60g each)
2 tablespoons chopped chives
tomato chutney, to serve

1 Spray a 4-hole (2-tablespoon) sausage roll maker with oil.

2 Cut pastry sheet in half. With the machine turned off, position a half pastry sheet to cover the four holes. Press pastry gently into holes. Fold 4 slices of ham in half; place 1 in each hole. Crack an egg into each hole. Season with salt and pepper.

3 Turn machine on. Close lid; cook for 10 minutes or until pastry is golden and egg is cooked. Transfer to a wire rack. Turn machine off for 5 minutes to cool slightly.

4 Repeat steps 3 and 4 with remaining half pastry sheet, ham and eggs to make 8 tarts in total. Use a sharp knife to cut batches into separate tarts.

5 Serve breakfast tarts topped with chives and tomato chutney.

COOK'S NOTES
You could use any kind of
leftover pasta you may have in
the fridge; you will need 300g.
This recipe is best made just
before serving.

CACIO E PEPE ROLLS

PREP + COOK TIME 25 MINUTES

300g packet microwave ready-cooked pasta spirals

200ml thickened cream

1 teaspoon finely ground black pepper

⅔ cup (50g) finely grated parmesan, plus extra to serve

2 eggs, beaten lightly

2 tablespoons finely chopped flat-leaf parsley, plus extra to serve

olive oil cooking spray

⅓ cup (25g) panko (japanese) breadcrumbs

20g butter, softened

lemon wedges, to serve

1 Heat pasta according to packet directions.

2 Bring cream to a simmer in a large deep frying pan over medium heat. Add pasta and pepper; cook, stirring, for 2 minutes or until sauce thickens and just coats the pasta. Turn off the heat. Add parmesan, egg and parsley; stir until well combined. Season. Cool slightly.

3 Spray a 4-hole (2-tablespoon) sausage roll maker with oil.

4 Fill each hole with ⅓ cup pasta mixture; top each with a rounded 1 teaspoon breadcrumbs and dots of butter. Turn machine on. Close lid; cook for 8 minutes or until rolls are golden brown and firm. Transfer to a baking-paper-lined tray; cover to keep warm. Turn machine off for 5 minutes to cool slightly. Repeat with remaining pasta mixture, breadcrumb mixture and butter to make 8 rolls in total.

5 Serve rolls hot topped with extra parmesan and parsley, and with lemon wedges.

MAKES MAKES MAKES MAKES 6

CHICKEN COUSCOUS TORTILLA ROLLS

PREP + COOK TIME 25 MINUTES

200g packet frozen pearl couscous with chickpeas and vegetables
6 x 20cm flour tortillas
1 cup (160g) coarsely chopped barbecue chicken
75g fetta, crumbled
2 teaspoons rose harissa paste (see Cook's Notes), plus extra to serve
½ cup fresh mint leaves
cooking oil spray
½ cup (140g) greek yoghurt

1 Heat couscous mix and tortillas according to packet directions.

2 Combine couscous mix, chicken, fetta, harissa and half the mint in a bowl; season.

3 Place a tortilla on a work surface; spoon 2 heaped tablespoons of chicken mixture on tortilla 4cm up from the bottom edge in a 10cm log shape. Fold bottom edge of tortilla over filling, roll over once; fold in the sides, then continue rolling to enclose filling. Repeat to make 6 rolls in total.

4 Spray a 4-hole (2-tablespoon) sausage roll maker with oil.

5 Place four rolls in holes; spray tops with oil. Turn machine on. Close lid; cook for 5 minutes or until golden. Transfer to a tray; cover to keep warm. Turn machine off for 5 minutes to cool slightly. Repeat with remaining rolls.

6 Meanwhile, finely chop remaining mint; combine with yoghurt in a small bowl. Season to taste.

7 Serve tortilla rolls topped with minted yoghurt and extra harissa.

***COOK'S NOTES** Rose harissa has the addition of rose petals and water which makes it less fiery. Adjust the amount of harissa depending on the type you use and your chilli tolerance level.*

COOK'S NOTES

Damper is best eaten on the day it is made. The secret to the best texture is not to overmix it; stir until the ingredients just come together.

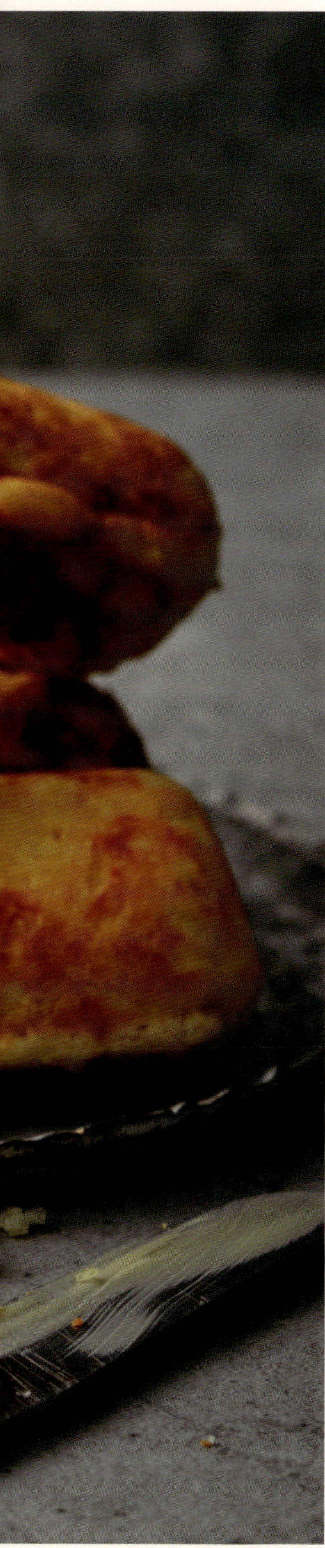

CHEESY DAMPER ROLLS

PREP + COOK TIME 30 MINUTES

2 cups (300g) self-raising flour
¼ teaspoon salt
50g cold butter, chopped
1 cup (80g) finely grated parmesan
1 cup (250ml) milk
cooking oil spray
salted butter, to serve

1 Combine sifted flour and salt in a large bowl. Rub in the butter with your fingertips until combined. Stir through ⅔ cup of the cheese. Add milk. Using a butter knife, 'cut' the milk through the flour mixture until combined.

2 Spray a 4-hole (2-tablespoon) sausage roll maker with oil.

3 Fill each hole with a ¼ cup of damper mixture. Sprinkle with half the remaining cheese. Turn machine on. Close lid; cook for 8 minutes or until browned and firm to touch. Transfer to a wire rack. Turn machine off for 5 minutes to cool slightly. Repeat with remaining damper mixture and cheese to make 8 rolls in total.

4 Serve damper rolls warm or cool with salted butter.

DAMPER ROLL VARIATIONS

CHEESE & FENNEL

Make Cheesy Damper Rolls (page 151), adding 1 teaspoon fennel seeds and 2 teaspoons mustard powder to the flour mixture. In step 3, top with another 1 teaspoon fennel seeds before sprinkling with cheese. Continue as directed.

OLIVE & ROSEMARY

Make Cheesy Damper Rolls (page 151), adding 1 tablespoon finely chopped fresh rosemary leaves and ¼ cup (40g) finely chopped pitted green olives to the flour mixture. In step 3, top rolls with another ¼ cup (40g) squashed pitted green olives and extra rosemary sprigs after sprinkling with cheese. Continue as directed.

SUNDRIED TOMATO, CHEESE & THYME

Make Cheesy Damper Rolls (page 151), adding 1 tablespoon fresh thyme leaves and ½ cup sliced sundried tomatoes to the flour mixture, and combining 1 tablespoon tomato paste with the milk. In step 3, top with ½ cup sliced sundried tomatoes and extra thyme sprigs after sprinkling with cheese, then cook for 1 minute less than directed.

RICE-FILLED ROMA TOMATOES

PREP + COOK TIME 55 MINUTES (+ COOLING)

6 large roma (egg) tomatoes (540g)
1 tablespoon extra virgin olive oil, plus extra to serve (optional)
1 small onion (100g), chopped finely
2 teaspoons ground cumin
250g packet microwave jasmine rice
1 small zucchini (90g), grated finely, squeezed dry
2 tablespoons pine nuts, toasted
100g haloumi, chopped finely
2 tablespoons finely chopped coriander, plus extra to serve
olive oil cooking spray
greek yoghurt, to serve

1 Cut roma tomatoes in half lengthways. Using a teaspoon, remove seeds and discard. Then using the teaspoon, scoop out the flesh to create a shell. Discard flesh.

2 Heat olive oil in a large frying pan over medium heat; cook onion, stirring, for 3 minutes or until softened. Add cumin; cook, stirring, for 1 minute or until fragrant. Add rice, zucchini and pine nuts; cook, stirring, for 3 minutes or until heated through. Remove from heat; stir in haloumi and coriander.

3 Spray a 4-hole (2-tablespoon) sausage roll maker with oil.

4 Using damp hands, press 2 heaped tablespoons of rice mixture into each tomato cavity.

5 Place four filled tomato halves into holes; spray tops with oil. Turn machine on. Close lid, without locking; cook for 10 minutes or until rice is golden brown and tomato is warmed through. Transfer to a tray; cover to keep warm. Turn machine off for 5 minutes to cool slightly. Repeat cooking in batches with remaining filled tomato halves.

6 Serve rice-filled tomatoes with yoghurt and extra chopped coriander, drizzled with a little extra olive oil.

2
1
4
7
8
9
6

DIY SAVOURY FILLINGS

Snacks and lunchbox treats can all be whipped up without any planning, utilising leftovers, pantry staples and anything your imagination can conjure. Here are some ideas of what's possible; simply stick to the 2-3 tablespoons of filling rule and cook until golden, turning rolls halfway through cooking time.

1 CONDIMENTS Dips (pesto, hummus, sundried tomato paste) and condiments (barbecue sauce, ketchup, mustard and mayonnaise) are your ally in flavouring leftovers and store cupboard staples. Just go easy on adding too much of them or they will ooze.

2 CANNED CORN KERNELS Likely there will be a can in the pantry or some frozen kernels (use from frozen) in the freezer; pair with luncheon meats, BBQ chicken or cheese for instant flavour pleasers.

3 CANNED BEANS For beans with sauces – baked beans, Mexi beans and the like – use alone or add a little grated cheese. For canned beans without a sauce, stir in a little bit of pasta sauce, barbecue sauce or tomato sauce to add a flavour profile.

4 MINI FRANKFURTS Just add baked beans for a two ingredient winning combo, swap the franks for ham for another flavour riff.

5 SLOW-COOKED MEATS Use leftover slow-cooked meats (or purchase) for tasty one-ingredient fillings. Bolognese and shredded chicken (with a sauce) also works well for fillings too.

6 CANNED FISH Canned salmon or tuna can be transformed into winning snack rolls. Pick a canned tuna with a flavour twist (smoked, chilli or lemon all work) to get even more bang for your roll buck. A little mayonnaise, white sauce or cheese will keep things saucy.

7 CHERRY TOMATOES Chopped or halved cherry tomatoes or ordinary tomatoes moisten other leftover ingredients. And it goes with out saying that any type of cheese is a perfect companion.

8 TORTILLAS Filled, rolled and with the ends tucked in, small tortillas become the vehicle for an instant toastie or roll.

9 FLAVOURED CHEESE STICKS What's better than melted cheese? Flavoured melted cheese sticks! These cheese sticks are the perfect size for your machine so all you'll need is the pastry.

GLOSSARY

ALMONDS
FLAKED paper-thin slices of blanched or natural almonds.
MEAL also known as ground almonds; powdered to a coarse flour-like texture.
NATURAL almond kernels with the brown skin on.

BAKING PAPER also called parchment or baking parchment; a silicone-coated paper that is primarily used for lining baking pans and oven trays so cooked food doesn't stick, making removal easy.

BAKING POWDER a raising agent consisting mainly of two parts cream of tartar to one part bicarbonate of soda (baking soda).

BASIL the most common type of basil; this herb is used extensively in Italian dishes and is one of the main ingredients in pesto.

BICARBONATE OF SODA also known as bicarb; a mild alkali used as a raising agent in baking.

BREADCRUMBS, PANKO (JAPANESE) available in two kinds: larger pieces and fine crumbs. They have a lighter texture than Western-style breadcrumbs. Available from Asian food stores and most supermarkets.

BROCCOLINI a cross between broccoli and chinese kale; it has long asparagus-like stems with a long loose floret, both are edible. Resembles broccoli but is milder and sweeter in taste.

BUTTER we use salted butter unless stated otherwise. Unsalted or 'sweet' butter has no salt added and is popular among pastry chefs.

CAPSICUM also known as bell pepper; comes in many colours: red, green, yellow and orange. Discard seeds and membranes before use.

CARDAMOM a spice native to India and used extensively in its cuisine; sold in the pod, as seeds or ground. Cardamom has a distinctive aromatic and sweetly rich flavour.

CHEESE
CREAM CHEESE commonly called Philadelphia or Philly; a soft cow's milk cheese, its fat content ranges from 14–33%.
FETTA Greek in origin; a crumbly textured goat's or sheep's milk cheese with a sharp, salty taste. Ripened and stored in salted whey.
GOAT'S made from goat's milk and has an earthy, strong taste. Available in soft, crumbly and firm textures, in various shapes and sizes, and sometimes rolled in ash or herbs.
MOZZARELLA soft, spun-curd cheese, originating in Southern Italy where it was traditionally made from water-buffalo milk. Now generally made from cow's milk, it is the most popular pizza cheese because of its low melting point and elasticity when heated.
PARMESAN also called parmigiano; is a hard, grainy cow-milk cheese originating in Italy. Reggiano is the best variety.
RICOTTA a soft, sweet, moist, white cow's milk cheese with a low fat content and a slightly grainy texture. The name roughly translates as 'cooked again' and refers to ricotta's manufacture from a whey that is itself a by-product of other cheese-making.

CHERRIES small, soft stone fruit. Sweet cherries are eaten whole and in desserts while sour cherries such as the morello variety are used for jams, preserves, pies and savoury dishes.

CHICKPEAS are an irregularly round, sandy-coloured legume; they have a firm texture even after cooking, a floury mouth-feel and robust nutty flavour. Available canned or dried.

CHILLI available in many types and sizes. Use rubber gloves when seeding and chopping fresh chillies as they can burn your skin. Removing membranes and seeds lessens the heat level.
GREEN any unripened chilli; also some particular varieties that are ripe when green, such as jalapeño, habanero, poblano or serrano.
JALAPEÑO (pronounced hah-lah-pain-yo) a fairly hot, medium-sized, plump, dark green chilli; available pickled (sold canned or bottled) and fresh.
LONG RED fresh and dried; a generic term used for any moderately hot, long chilli (about 6-8cm long).

CHINESE FIVE SPICE POWDER a fragrant mixture of ground cinnamon, cloves, star anise, sichuan pepper and fennel seeds. Used in Chinese and other Asian cooking; available from most supermarkets or Asian food shops.

CHOCOLATE
DARK also known as semi-sweet; made of a high percentage of cocoa liquor and cocoa butter, and a little added sugar.

MILK most popular eating chocolate, mild and very sweet; similar in make-up to dark chocolate with the difference being the addition of milk solids.
WHITE contains no cocoa solids but derives its sweet flavour from cocoa butter. It is very sensitive to heat.

CINNAMON available in pieces (sticks or quills) and ground into powder; one of the world's most common spices, used as a sweet, fragrant flavouring for both sweet and savoury foods.

COCONUT
DESICCATED concentrated, dried, unsweetened and finely shredded coconut flesh.
FLAKED dried flaked coconut flesh.
MILK not the liquid inside the fruit (coconut water), but the diluted liquid from the second pressing of the white flesh of a mature coconut (the first pressing produces coconut cream). Available in cans and cartons at most supermarkets.
SHREDDED unsweetened thin strips of dried coconut flesh.

CORNFLOUR made from corn (100% maize) or wheat; used as a thickening agent in cooking.

COUSCOUS a fine, dehydrated, grain-like cereal product made from semolina; it swells to three or four times its original size when liquid is added. It is eaten like rice with a tagine, as a side dish or salad ingredient.

CREAM, THICKENED a whipping cream containing a thickener. Minimum fat content 35%.

CRÈME FRAÎCHE a mature, naturally fermented cream with a velvety texture and slightly tangy, nutty flavour. Minimum fat content 35%. A French variation of sour cream, it boils without curdling and is used in sweet and savoury dishes.

CUMIN also called zeera or comino; resembling caraway in size, cumin is the dried seed of a plant related to the parsley family. Its spicy, almost curry-like flavour is essential to the traditional foods of Mexico, India, North Africa and the Middle East. Available dried as seeds or ground.

EGGPLANT also called aubergine. Ranges in size from tiny to very large and in colour from pale green to deep purple. Can also be purchased char-grilled, packed in oil, in jars.

EGGWASH beaten egg (white, yolk or both) and milk or water; often brushed over pastry to impart colour or gloss.

FENNEL a white to very pale green-white, firm, crisp, roundish vegetable about 8-12cm in diameter. The bulb has a slightly sweet, anise flavour but the leaves have a much stronger taste.

FLOUR
PLAIN a general all-purpose unbleached wheat flour.
SELF-RAISING plain flour sifted with baking powder; make at home in the proportion of 1 cup flour to 2 teaspoons baking powder.

GINGER
FRESH also called green or root ginger; the thick gnarled root of a tropical plant.
GROUND used as a flavouring in baking but cannot be substituted for fresh ginger.

GOLDEN SYRUP a by-product of refined sugarcane; pure maple syrup or honey can be substituted. Treacle is a similar product, however, it is more viscous and has a stronger flavour and aroma than golden syrup (which has been refined further and contains fewer impurities).

HARISSA a Moroccan paste made from dried chillies, cumin, garlic, oil and caraway seeds. Available from Middle Eastern food shops and supermarkets.

MAPLE SYRUP distilled from the sap of sugar maple trees found only in Canada and the USA. Maple-flavoured syrup or pancake syrup is not an adequate substitute for the real thing.

MASCARPONE an Italian fresh cultured-cream product made in much the same way as yoghurt. Whiteish to creamy yellow in colour, it has a buttery-rich, luscious texture. Soft, creamy and spreadable, it is used in Italian desserts and as an accompaniment to fresh fruit.

MUSTARD, DIJON pale brown, distinctively flavoured, mild french mustard.

NUTMEG a strong and pungent spice from the dried nut of an evergreen tree native to Indonesia. Usually found ground but the flavour is more intense from a whole nut, available from spice shops, so it's best to grate your own. Used most often in baking and desserts, but also works nicely in savoury dishes.

OIL

OLIVE made from ripened olives. Extra virgin and virgin are the first and second press, respectively, of the olives; "extra light" or "light" on other types refers to taste not fat levels.

PEANUT pressed from ground peanuts; most commonly used oil in Asian cooking because of its capacity to handle high heat without burning (high smoke point).

SESAME used as a flavouring rather than in cooking.

ONIONS

GREEN also called, incorrectly, shallot; an immature onion picked before the bulb has formed, has a long, bright-green stalk.

RED also known as spanish, red spanish or bermuda onion; a sweet-flavoured, large, purple-red onion.

SHALLOTS also called french or golden shallots or eschalots; small and brown-skinned.

SPRING an onion with a small white bulb and long, narrow green-leafed tops.

PASTRY

FILLO paper-thin sheets of raw pastry; brush each sheet with oil or melted butter, stack in layers, then cut and fold as directed.

SHEETS ready-rolled packaged sheets of frozen puff and shortcrust pastry, available from supermarkets.

PINE NUTS not a nut but a small, cream-coloured kernel from pine cones. Toast before use to bring out their flavour.

POMEGRANATE MOLASSES not to be confused with pomegranate syrup or grenadine (used in cocktails); pomegranate molasses is thicker, browner, and more concentrated in flavour — tart and sharp, slightly sweet and fruity. Brush over grilling or roasting meat, seafood or poultry, add to salad dressings or sauces. Buy from Middle Eastern food stores or specialty food shops.

RHUBARB long, green-red stalks become sweet and edible when cooked. The leaves are toxic, therefore not edible; trim off and discard the leaves before cutting the stalks.

ROASTING/TOASTING desiccated coconut, pine nuts and sesame seeds toast more evenly if stirred over low heat in a heavy-based frying pan; their natural oils will help turn them golden. Remove them from the pan immediately. Nuts and dried coconut can be roasted in the oven to release their aromatic essential oils. Spread evenly onto an oven tray, roast at 180°C/350°F for about 5 minutes.

SESAME SEEDS black and white are the most common of this small oval seed, however there are also red and brown varieties. Used as an ingredient and as a condiment.

SPINACH also called english spinach and incorrectly, silverbeet. Baby spinach leaves are eaten raw in salads or cooked until wilted.

SUGAR

BROWN very soft, finely granulated sugar retaining molasses for its characteristic colour and flavour.

CASTER finely granulated table sugar.

DEMERARA small-grained golden-coloured crystal sugar.

ICING also called powdered sugar; pulverised granulated sugar crushed with a little cornflour.

WHITE coarse, granulated table sugar, also known as crystal sugar.

TOFU also called bean curd; an off-white, custard-like product made from the "milk" of crushed soybeans. Comes fresh as soft or firm, and processed as fried or pressed dried sheets. Fresh tofu can be refrigerated in water (changed daily) for up to 4 days.

TOMATOES

BOTTLED PASTA SAUCE a prepared sauce; a blend of tomatoes, herbs and spices.

SEMI-DRIED partially dried tomato pieces in olive oil; softer and juicier than sun-dried, these are not a preserve thus do not keep as long as sun-dried.

VANILLA

EXTRACT made by extracting the flavour from the vanilla bean pod; pods are soaked, usually in alcohol, to capture the authentic flavour.

PASTE made from vanilla pods and contains real seeds. Is highly concentrated; 1 teaspoon replaces a whole vanilla pod. Found in most supermarkets in the baking section.

YOGHURT, GREEK plain yoghurt strained in a cloth (muslin) to remove the whey and to give it a creamy consistency.

ZUCCHINI also called courgette; small dark-green or yellow vegetable of the squash family.

CONVERSION CHART

MEASURES

One Australian metric measuring cup holds approximately 250ml; one Australian metric tablespoon holds 20ml; one Australian metric teaspoon holds 5ml.

North America, New Zealand and the United Kingdom use a 15ml tablespoon. The difference between one country's measuring cups and another's is within a two- or three-teaspoon variance and will not affect your results.

All cup and spoon measurements are level unless noted otherwise.

The most accurate way of measuring dry ingredients is to weigh them.

When measuring liquids, use a clear glass or plastic jug with the metric markings.

We use extra-large eggs with an average weight of 60g.

DRY MEASURES

metric	imperial
15g	½oz
30g	1oz
60g	2oz
90g	3oz
125g	4oz (¼lb)
155g	5oz
185g	6oz
220g	7oz
250g	8oz (½lb)
280g	9oz
315g	10oz
345g	11oz
375g	12oz (¾lb)
410g	13oz
440g	14oz
470g	15oz
500g	16oz (1lb)
750g	24oz (1½lb)
1kg	32oz (2lb)

OVEN TEMPERATURES

The oven temperatures in this book are for conventional ovens.
If you use a fan-forced oven, reduce the temperature by 10-20 degrees.

	°C (Celsius)	°F (Fahrenheit)
Very slow	120	250
Slow	150	300
Moderately slow	160	325
Moderate	180	350
Moderately hot	200	400
Hot	220	425
Very hot	240	475

LIQUID MEASURES

metric	imperial
30ml	1 fluid oz
60ml	2 fluid oz
100ml	3 fluid oz
125ml	4 fluid oz
150ml	5 fluid oz
190ml	6 fluid oz
250ml	8 fluid oz
300ml	10 fluid oz
500ml	16 fluid oz
600ml	20 fluid oz
1000ml (1 litre)	1¾ pints

LENGTH MEASURES

metric	imperial
3mm	⅛in
6mm	¼in
1cm	½in
2cm	¾in
2.5cm	1in
5cm	2in
6cm	2½in
8cm	3in
10cm	4in
13cm	5in
15cm	6in
18cm	7in
20cm	8in
22cm	9in
25cm	10in
28cm	11in
30cm	12in (1ft)

INDEX

Published in 2022 by Are Media Books, Australia.
Are Media Books is a division of Are Media Pty Limited.

Are Media

Chief Executive Officer
Jane Huxley

Are Media Books

Group Publisher Nicole Byers

Editorial & Food Director
Sophia Young

Creative Director Hannah Blackmore

Managing Editor Stephanie Kistner

Art Director & Designer
Jeannel Cunanan

Food Editor Sophia Young

Head of Operations David Scotto

Photographer Con Poulos

Stylist Olivia Blackmore

Photochefs
Rebecca Lyall, Clare Maguire

Assistant Photochef Caitlyn McGrath

Recipe Developers
Rebecca Lyall, Clare Maguire

womensweeklyfood

@womensweeklyfood

Printed in China by
1010 Printing International

A catalogue record for this
book is available from the
National Library of Australia.

ISBN 978-1-92586-690-2 : paperback

Published by Are Media Books,
a division of Are Media Pty Limited,
54 Park St, Sydney; GPO Box 4088,
Sydney, NSW 2001, Australia
Ph +61 2 9282 8000
www.awwcookbooks.com.au

International rights enquiries
internationalrights@aremedia.com.au

Order books
phone 1300 322 007 (within Australia)

or order online at
www.awwcookbooks.com.au

Send recipe enquiries to
recipeenquiries@aremedia.com.au